Northwest Landscaping

A PRACTICAL GUIDE TO CREATING THE GARDEN YOU'VE ALWAYS WANTED

MICHAEL MUNRO

Alaska Northwest Books™

ANCHORAGE ◆ SEATTLE

Library of Congress Cataloging-in-Publication Data
Munro, Michael, 1949–
        Northwest landscaping : a practical guide to creating the
    garden you've always wanted / by Michael Munro.
                        p.   cm.
        Includes bibliographical references and index.
        ISBN 0-88240-393-1
        1. Landscape architecture — Northwest, Pacific. 2.
    Landscape gardening — Northwest, Pacific. I. Title.
    SB473.M82   1992
    712'.6'09795 — dc20   91-45935
                                                                CIP

Project editor: Carolyn Smith
Editors: Alice Copp Smith and Shellie Tucker
Book and cover designers: Elizabeth Watson and Cameron Mason
Illustrator: Mike Kowalski

All photographs by the author.

Front cover: Colorful Adirondack-style chairs brighten up a shady
area off the front porch in a design by landscape architect Keith
Geller. *Back cover* (see photos and captions, pp. 80–90, for complete
images and descriptions): *(clockwise from top)* Landscape designs by
Withey-Price Landscape Design, Jerry Munro, Gil Schieber,
Withey-Price Landscape Design, and Bill Munro. Garden designs
on pp. 62 and 75 are by Withey-Price Landscape Design.

Alaska Northwest Books™
A division of GTE Discovery Publications, Inc.
22026 20th Avenue S.E.
Bothell, WA 98021

Printed in the United States of America

For Irene,

Sarah, and Daniel—

gardeners three

Acknowledgments

I am truly grateful to the following landscape professionals, homeowners, and amateur garden enthusiasts for their information, assistance, and patience while I was writing this book: Sue Buckles, head gardener, Children's Hospital and Medical Center, and Alden Buckles; Darcy Crane, Crane Design; Keith Geller, landscape architect; Kristan Johnson, landscape contractor, Abundant Landscape Design; Rick Kyper, landscape contractor; R. Scott Lankford, landscape architect, Lankford Associates; George "Bud" Merrill, landscape architect; Bill Munro, landscape contractor, Rose Hill Landscaping; Jerry Munro, nursery owner, Munro's Nursery; Karen Munro, nursery owner, Edwards Nursery, Moses Lake; Charles Price and Glenn Withey, Withey-Price Landscape and Design Services; Douglas Reymore, general contractor, Cascade Construction; Gilbert Schieber, horticulturist and garden designer, Good Shepherd Nursery, and head groundskeeper, Good Shepherd Center; Cass Turnbull Gardening Services, PlantAmnesty,

Gardener's Referral Service; and Rosann Benedict, Joan Flakus, Mr. and Mrs. John Hepburn, Daniel Jilka, Margaret Leahy, Ed Mirabella, Frederick J. Rahn II, and Robert and Barbara Story.

Thanks as well to the staff at Alaska Northwest Books™ for their encouragement and expertise: editors Marlene Blessing, Carolyn Smith, and Shellie Tucker; Elizabeth Watson and Cameron Mason for their design skills; and editor-in-the-trenches Alice Copp Smith, who knows editing and plants.

Thanks to Mike Kowalski for his ability to turn my words and gestures into pictures that speak.

And thanks also to: Chris Merrill and Sally Abella for reading early drafts of this book and for making suggestions; Floyd Lee for photographic advice; Lisa Hummell; Mike Yigena; Mrs. Milton Walker of the Walker Rock Garden; Tory Galloway of Victoria Gardens; Ike Binford; Carrie Becker; Bob McGilvray; Douglas and Joal Johnson; Al and Doris Foster; the Association for Women in Landscaping; and the Northwest Perennial Alliance.

Contents

Landscaping—Northwest Style

Landscaping your own yard can be fun and rewarding—the results can look wonderful and you can save lots of money. But where do you start? How do you create a garden that reflects your personal vision and meets your landscaping needs? Doing it yourself can be especially daunting if you are unfamiliar with basic design concepts and construction techniques. You could end up spending a good deal of time and money creating something you don't like and can't use. The aim of this book is to encourage the landscaper, whether novice or experienced, to tackle his or her own yard. In the pages that follow, we'll discuss all stages of landscape design and construction—from developing a plan to realizing it, with a special emphasis on incorporating plants and materials best suited to our region. Although the design and construction techniques covered here can be applied most anywhere else in the country, your ability to create a successful landscape will be enhanced when you learn what this region has to offer and how to use it.

We in the Northwest are the beneficiaries of a horticultural cornucopia that makes us the envy of gardeners in other parts of the country. Certainly the region's climate and terrain influence which plants and materials we choose to use in our landscapes. West of the Cascade Range, the warming influence of the Pacific Ocean's Japan Current creates a far milder climate than might be expected, considering our northern latitude: not too hot in summer, not too cold in winter. East of the Cascade mountains, away from that moderating current, temperature extremes are much greater. Together, the two distinct climates in the Northwest have given rise to an astonishing range of plants and trees.

We also draw inspiration from an impressive array of natural features. Water is a shaping element in the Northwest: deep mountain lakes, cascading rivers, and the moody Pacific. We have rolling hills that folks from other regions call mountains. And we have real mountains that you can't walk up for a casual hike—volcanoes, ice-covered ruptures of the skyline, spectacular masses of tilted and fractured rock. Where else can you find a rain forest within an hour's drive of a dry "banana belt," or a windswept seashore twenty miles from an alpine meadow? Where else can you have breakfast amid cool, ancient evergreens, then drive for lunch among sagebrush and dust devils?

Mix this rich assortment of native plant life and varied terrain, and you have a good recipe for Northwest-style landscaping: informal, naturalistic groupings of plants, rocks, weathered wood, a hint of water, and not a straight line in sight—all arranged to suggest scenes you might find in the wilderness.

But there is more to Northwest landscaping than an echoing of these regional elements. Outside influences have shaped landscaping in the Northwest as well. The climate of the maritime Northwest is much like that of England, Japan, and parts of Europe, and our designs and plant choices often incorporate the styles of those regions. In Japanese gardens, there is careful consideration for placement of plants and stone. Emphasis is on the form, texture, and shape of plantings; the palette is often muted. The combination of elements can create a highly stylized representation of a scene from nature. English gardens, in a profusion of flowering color set against foliage textures, emphasize an appreciation for plant variety. And when the architecture of our houses encourages it, even formal European landscaping can be appropriate for some Northwest yards.

Depending on the climate in our particular neighborhood of the Northwest, we can, and do, grow plants that have originated in near-arctic to near-tropical parts of the world. Within the pages of this book, you'll see and read about plants from Australia, New Zealand, South America, and most of North America, from California to the Yukon, all thriving in Northwest landscapes. In my own yard near Seattle, I'm able to grow crinums from Africa, hardy orchids from Asia, rhododendrons from Japan and the Himalayas, foxgloves from England, and herbs from the Mediterranean, all in the shelter of native Western red cedars and bigleaf maples. This variety of plantings would not be possible in many other parts of the country. If you enjoy experimenting with plants, chances are you can readily find less common varieties to plant in your yard. Many local nurseries are run by enthusiasts who champion unusual plants rather than concentrate on the more familiar types.

There can be drawbacks to this abundance, though. With all the plants and landscaping options available, it can be difficult to make the right choices, even if you know something about plants. And if you're a real beginner, it might be downright intimidating.

This book is meant to help you try, by providing you with practical and realistic ways to create and install your own landscaping. Perhaps because of the Northwest's relatively recent pioneer past, people here seem especially inclined to want to get outside and move the earth. Also, landscaping traditions in the Northwest are not firmly entrenched; there is still room for experimentation and change. Even when we adapt themes from other regions, we bring to our landscapes an attitude that distinguishes our gardens. This attitude includes:

- A wide interest in gardening. Beautiful landscapes are not the sole province of the wealthy here; almost anyone with a spot of land can create a pleasing yard.

- A strong do-it-yourself streak. We do our own

landscaping not just to save money, but also because of the real sense of accomplishment we get in return.

◆ A deep commitment to the environment. Whether hiking in the wilderness or recycling yard waste, we're conscious of caring for and preserving the region's great natural beauty.

Based on my experiences as a landscaper in the Northwest for over twenty years, and as an instructor of a do-it-yourself home landscaping course at the University of Washington's Experimental College, I have learned that even horticultural novices can accomplish wonders in their yards—if they have straightforward procedures to follow. I'll guide you through each step, from the initial assessment of your wants and needs, through the design phase, and into the actual construction and planting of your yard. You'll learn what kinds of projects you might want to take on by yourself and when to call for help from professionals. You'll learn which landscape features will haunt you with excessive maintenance demands. And you'll see how both professional and amateur designers have created landscapes that are both aesthetic and practical.

When you finish this book you'll be ready to create a yard that is attractive, affordable, and maintainable—and fulfills your current and future needs. Remember that your yard is a living, evolving thing. I encourage you to take at least as long to plan your landscape as you do to build it. The process can be just as satisfying as the end result. And don't be surprised if your landscaping efforts give you a new way of looking at your surroundings and a deeper appreciation for the natural world. That can be part of the reward, too. I invite you to begin the process of landscaping your own yard—Northwest style.

CHAPTER ONE

Chasing a Vision

*Identifying Your
Landscaping Wants, Needs,
and Options*

*Y*ou're thinking about doing something to your yard, and you have your reasons. Maybe you're ready to take up gardening as a serious hobby; maybe you're tired of seeing your neighbors shake their heads as they pass by; maybe your yard just doesn't meet your needs.

13

How to Begin

MAKING A LIST: So where do you start? Not at your local nursery, I hope—unless you leave your checkbook at home. That comes later. It's much safer to start with a sheet of paper and a pencil. You don't even need to draw a sketch of your yard yet. Begin with a list. Do some blue-sky thinking about what you really want from your yard. Be idealistic, be unrealistic, be inventive. Would you like to have a wildlife sanctuary? Write it down. Would you like to have topiary plants? Write it down. A children's play area? An orchard? A pond filled with koi? Write it all down. Ask other members of your family to contribute ideas, and corral your friends and get their ideas as well.

What you are doing now is sending up trial balloons. Some of them may be ridiculous—too expensive, too much work, inappropriate for your yard or your lifestyle—but that's all right. Right now you need to generate ideas. Reality will intrude soon enough. Most of us will run out of money or yard before we run out of ideas. It's best to start with too many ideas rather than too few, just as it's more rewarding to thin out exuberant seedlings growing in fertile soil than to urge on weaklings struggling in clay. With your ideas on paper, you may notice how some of them clash when together on the same page and, conversely, how some less-obvious thoughts start to shine.

REFINING THE LIST: Now that you have a list of your own landscape wishes, you might want to compare it with some thoughts that other people— landscape students and clients—have expressed to me over the years, which I outline below. If you like, blend the most appealing of these ideas into your own list. When you're done, it's time to begin narrowing the list and setting priorities.

Typical Reasons for Landscaping

PLEASURE: People need a place to play. Being indoors is fine on rainy winter days, but when the sun shines, it feels good to get out. How do you envision using your yard? Do you have children? Then they need a place where they can do things without endangering themselves or the shrubbery: a lawn area, a patio with a basketball hoop on one side, a swing or climbing set, a sandbox.

Grown-ups sometimes need outdoor room too. You might need room for some patio or lawn chairs, or a hot tub or a pool.

Do you like cut flowers? Maybe there could be room for a cutting garden in your yard.

Do you like plants a lot and have some time to devote to them? Maybe you would enjoy doing some ongoing horticulture as a hobby.

Do you get aesthetic pleasure out of viewing a well-done garden? Concentrating on design elements will help to make your garden beautiful.

But what if you hate the thought of getting out in the yard to take care of it? If you can afford to have someone else maintain it, so much the better; but if not, you may want to write *"low maintenance"* on your list of landscape design requirements. What constitutes a low-maintenance yard? As a practical rule, if your yard takes more effort to keep in shape than you're willing to give it, then it's a high-maintenance yard. If you don't mind the amount of work you put into it, then it's low-maintenance. People have their own levels of tolerance for different kinds of work too. Some people would rather mow lawns for three hours a week than weed flower beds for thirty minutes. See Chapter 5, "Maintenance: Planning with Upkeep in Mind," for information about how much maintenance work different parts of the landscape may take.

ECONOMICS: Some people landscape their yards with the expectation that they will get tangible rewards for doing so. Sometimes they are right.

If you intend to sell your house anytime soon, a bit of strategic yard work can make your house sell faster, but it won't automatically translate into a higher selling price. What will pay off best? Start with neatness. Weed the flower beds, rake up leaves and debris, carefully prune existing trees and shrubs. Then consider renewing flower-bed mulches and, perhaps, planting some cheap and colorful annuals if the season is right. Even though your efforts may not raise the selling price of your house, most real estate agents I've talked to agree that a well-maintained yard makes a house more inviting and easier to sell.

You are most likely to recoup any major landscaping investment, however, if you plant years before you plan to move. The plantings, if you take care of them, will increase in value, and you'll get the benefit of looking at a beautiful yard for all those years.

Fruit trees, berry bushes, and a vegetable garden can all produce some economic reward too. Let's be honest, though. If you expect to grow a significant portion of the food you eat, you must also expect to spend a certain amount of time working at it. Although it's possible to grow fruit trees and bushes with minimal effort, you are likely to get minimal crops if you do. (See "Edible Plants" in the Appendix for lists of plants that are both edible and decorative.)

There is yet another economic reason for doing your own landscaping: It should save you considerable money over the cost of hiring someone else to do it for you. Even if you decide to hire outside contractors to do certain parts of the work, you could save money by doing some parts of it yourself. Using the rule of thumb that half the cost of landscaping goes for labor and the other half for materials, you could

◆

Doing your own landscaping should save you considerable money over the cost of hiring someone to do it for you.

◆

save as much as 50 percent. With careful planning you could save a lot more than that. On the other hand, if you don't put much thought into the planning and execution, then you are wasting time and money by doing the work yourself and could even detract from the value of your home. When I started writing this book, I had an urge to include examples, complete with photographic evidence, of landscaping projects that started with good intentions and then went astray, but kinder impulses prevailed. Instead, I will point out later in the book the relative ease or difficulty of particular landscape projects, and caution you about some of the pitfalls along the way.

A house—and the yard that goes with it—can be a very visible expression of a family's aspirations and attitudes.

ADDITIONAL LANDSCAPE CONCERNS: Beyond pleasure and economics, there are many other reasons people landscape their yards. Certainly privacy is important. People who live in houses instead of apartments do so because they enjoy stretching their elbows without having the neighbors looking on all the time.

Safety rates high as a concern too. Maybe you want to keep your young children out of the street; perhaps you want to keep your neighbor's pit bull— or your neighbor—out of your yard. A pool or hot tub in your yard should also raise some safety concerns.

Security is important as well. You might want to place shrubs, trees, and landscape structures so they do not block windows or doors from the view of neighbors. There could be times when you appreciate having neighbors who keep an eye on things.

Do you see a conflict between a need for privacy and a need for security? Sometimes there can be, and you might have to juggle those conflicting needs.

There are other considerations. Do you avoid your patio in the summer because it gets too hot? It's possible that you need a shade tree there, or for the house itself.

I haven't yet mentioned ecology. It's ironic that gardening, which so many of us do because of a need to be with nature, can sometimes do more harm than good to the environment. The plantings you put in your yard, and the chemicals, water, and other materials you use to maintain them, have a direct effect on the environment. There are steps you can take, though, to make sure your efforts have a positive and not a negative effect.

Finally, think of your own personal style as you contemplate landscaping. A house—and the yard that goes with it—can be a very visible expression of a family's aspirations and attitudes. Viewed together (as they will be anyway), a house and yard may appear unremarkable, blending invisibly into the background; they may look bold and sharply personal, even eccentric; or they may look dowdy and tattered around the edges. Whether you intend it or not, your residence and its surroundings are your year-round public-relations department. Look to Chapter 6, "Design Principles," and Chapter 7, "Visions of the Garden," for some ways to make your landscaping reflect your personal tastes and vision. Then your residence will speak with your voice instead of talking behind your back.

Constraints on Landscaping

This is a good time to balance your landscape ideas with a dash of cold reality. There are five major elements that can limit your landscaping: time, money, available materials, interest, and talent. None of these is infinite. You need to take inventory of all of them—but unlike the "wants" list you made earlier, try to make this "have" list as realistic as possible.

TIME: Nobody has unlimited time to spend working on his or her yard. Most people have families, jobs, school, friends, hobbies. You are going to need two kinds of time: time to construct and time to maintain. First, try to estimate how much time you can spare for installing your landscape and then for keeping it up. Then estimate for each project you have in mind how much time it will take to do—and then to maintain. I would be very surprised if your available time matches the potential demands on your time, unless you are retired. I would encourage you to prune back your aspirations to match your resources. It doesn't make sense to reach a point where you resent the time you spend on your yard.

What's the answer, then? Set priorities among your projects, putting the most important or the most doable ones first. If you are starting with bare, exposed soil on a new lot, then grading, retaining walls (if needed), and soil preparation may take priority, followed by selection and planting of trees. Or perhaps a fence around the yard is your most pressing need. If you're moving into a house with established landscaping, then pruning, cleanup, and other yard resuscitation might top your list. The priorities will depend upon your particular situation.

Unless you have had experience with a similar yard in the past, you might have difficulty determining how much time it will take for upkeep of different parts of the landscape. Chapter 5, "Maintenance," offers help in evaluating how much time various features will take to maintain. Although plenty of surveys say we are entering a time of increased attention to family and home and decreased attention to careers, this claim may not be much comfort to you as you struggle to keep your yard looking good. I sometimes tell people to estimate how much time they think they are willing to devote to taking care of the yard, and then to divide that by three. I see too many ambitious projects, installed with care, that become abandoned as a family's interests change.

MONEY: Money limits most of us. Cost can affect the type or quantity of materials we use or the size of plants we buy. If your budget is tight, I suggest you use plants that will be an appropriate size when mature and consider skimping on initial size, rather than substituting cheaper, faster-growing species that will cause problems later. For nonliving elements of the landscape, such as fences and patios, you might have to make compromises or wait until you can afford the features you really want. The one place where I really urge you to be generous is in soil preparation. Short-changing the soil will haunt you for as long as you live in your house; you'll eventually pay in extra fertilizer costs, impaired plant health, and increased problems and maintenance related to insect and disease attacks. (See Chapter 8, "Site Preparation," for guidance on soil evaluation and preparation.)

What if you are one of those people who can easily afford to hire someone to design and landscape their yard? Doesn't it make more sense to simply do that and skip the self-education in home landscaping? Yes, but consider two factors. The first is personal style. If you view landscaping as a reflection of your own personality and values, you will want to participate actively in the planning phase. Second, there's the issue of consumer awareness. If you plan to entrust the landscape design and construction to others, you'll be better able to choose the firms carefully if you already speak some of the same language.

Every area of commerce—from music equipment to computers—has its own jargon, and if you buy before learning the dialect, you could end up with a snow job.

AVAILABLE MATERIALS: Available materials are wherever you find them. This could mean existing things in your yard: plants, topsoil, patios, fences. It could also mean donation of plant material from friends' and relatives' yards. It should also mean the nurseries and building supply places nearby. You may want to use their range of offerings as a guide to what plants and materials are suitable for your area. Don't expect to find totally suitable plants in the temporary "nursery" that pops up for a few weeks each spring in your grocery store's parking lot, though. A high percentage of parking-lot landscape material is trucked in from California nurseries, and may not be winter-hardy or acclimatized to our growing conditions. My favorite grocery-store plant joke is the colorful but tender South African heath (*Erica persoluta* and related species) that is typically mislabeled "Scotch heather" and therefore gets planted outside by people who mistakenly assume it is hardy. The joke sours when I see it sold at a major nursery chain too.

Many local arboreta and plant societies have sales that could augment your plantings, and other plant societies may have economical seed exchanges by mail. Don't forget the commercial mail-order seed

NOW FOR SOME self-assessment of another kind. Available abilities involve more than just skill at designing and doing. You also need to look carefully at your own physical strength and limitations. Some aspects of landscaping can be physically demanding or even hazardous. Many power tools carry warnings designed to protect those consumers who bother to read them. But not everything can be warning-labeled. You probably won't see cautions on your wheelbarrow warning you not to carry more weight than you can manage, but if you overdo it, your back will tell you the next morning. The same is true for moving railroad ties, shrubs, landscape rocks, or any other heavy object by hand. Impatience is your enemy. My own worst injuries have come from working with unfamiliar equipment, and from trying to finish up projects when I was too tired, or didn't have the proper tools or enough helping hands.

You can maximize your personal safety by following some general rules:

- Work at a steady pace; avoid rushing.
- Work in the cool of the day.
- Watch how you lift objects and how much you lift. To lift anything heavy, use a dolly from a rental shop, use leverage, or get lots of help.
- Heavy machinery, such as a tractor or bulldozer, requires special skills for efficient use. Even if you can handle a bulldozer safely, can you use it in a cost-effective manner?
- Leave tree removal to the experts. If I want to cut a tree down in a residential area, I don't try to cut it myself. I know how to do it, but I won't. I hire a bonded company and pay to have it done safely. It costs more, but I don't mind. I promised myself this after one prayerful moment spent watching a large alder lay itself down next to a customer's house.
- Use protection when appropriate: goggles for the eyes, earplugs for the ears, a face mask to filter out irritating dust from bark mulch or fresh cement, and heavy leather gloves. Even on hot days, I prefer to wear heavy boots and full-length jeans, and sometimes even a long-sleeved shirt. You should give special consideration to sunscreens and head protection too.
- If you are susceptible to repetitive stress injury, carpal tunnel syndrome, and the like, avoid using tools that will shake or jar your arms, such as weed whackers, chain saws, and power or manual hedge trimmers. You might also have to experiment cautiously with hammers, shovels, rakes, and most other commonly used gardening tools. If you have arthritis, you should look into gear- or ratchet-driven loppers and pruners; some trowels and weed forks have grips designed for people with limited hand mobility. If your garden and budget are large enough to justify the expense, consider buying a small garden tractor instead of just a wheelbarrow to help move materials. Or at least look into a garden cart with dual oversized wheels. They are inherently more stable when loaded than wheelbarrows.
- If you have limited mobility, plan your landscaping to maximize safe passage and minimize maintenance chores.

and plant companies, either. Take their offerings with a grain of salt, though. The colorful pictures and enthusiastic prose may encourage you to buy some things that look better in print than in real life—especially in the gray winter season when we would all happily be fools for visions of the colorful spring to come. An excellent source catalog for mail-order seed and plant companies is Barbara Barton's *Gardening by Mail: A Source Book* (Houghton Mifflin, 1990. See the Reading List at the back of this book).

Colorful pictures and enthusiastic prose may encourage you to buy some things that look better in print than in real life.

If you are interested in growing vegetables and flowers from seed, take a particularly close look at the seed companies that cater to our Northwest climate. These include Territorial Seed Company, Abundant Life Seed Foundation, Ed Hume, Nichols Garden Nursery, and Solly's Choice, among others. Some of these firms sell primarily by mail order, while others have seed racks throughout the region.

Local fanciers of "Dutch" bulbs have been pleased to discover they don't have to travel all the way to The Netherlands to see test gardens and growing fields. A great number of transplanted bulb growers from Holland have turned large swaths of the Puyallup, Fraser, and Skagit valleys into rich bulb-growing fields; for weeks every spring, the nearby towns and roads become clogged with sightseers of tulips and daffodils.

It's good to know sources for nonplant material too. Topsoils, soil amendments, and mulches might come from topsoil or bark companies, wood products yards or sawmills, or from trucking companies. Building, lumber, or landscape supply yards can be good sources of railroad ties, timbers, pavers, bricks, and modular building blocks. Sprinkler and irrigation parts will come from plumbing or irrigation supply houses. And if you are interested in garden decorations, you might want to visit some art galleries or sculptor's studios—or make the round of antique shops and yard sales. Many nurseries also carry decorative objects, such as birdbaths, birdhouses, and statuary.

Not all available materials are useful materials. Just because something is already in your yard doesn't mean you have to live with it. Read Chapter 3, "Taking Stock," for help in deciding what materials are worth keeping.

Beware, too, the housewarming gift with leaves and roots. The nice thing about normal unwanted gifts is that you can return them, or at worst stuff them in the attic and forget about them. Plant gifts, though, too often get planted no matter how inappropriate they are. If you are ever tempted to be a plant-giver, consider a gift certificate or—if that appears too cold—a gift of annuals in baskets. I sometimes think it would be nice to have a gardening registry for new homeowners at the local nursery, just as brides-to-be have registries at the local department store. Family and friends could choose the plants you needed from a plan you'd already made up.

INTEREST: Match your landscape schemes with your true level of interest. My experience suggests that gardens most often fail because the owners were talked into something grandiose and their interest petered out before the project was completed, or soon after. Sometimes homeowners run into technical problems and become discouraged. Or the maintenance keeps sneaking up on them, because they're dealing with a living, growing, dynamic environment. There's a lot of difference between wallpaper and wallflowers. When a yard looks abandoned before the people move out, I know they have been overwhelmed. If you aren't sure of your level of interest, it's safer to stick with the basics. Start simply and add later if you wish.

TALENT: Talent comes in two varieties—designing and doing. The best home landscapes reveal an artist's vision and an artisan's touch. There is wisdom in knowing how much natural talent you have, and when to look elsewhere for help.

It might be easier to assess your "doing" skills than your "designing" skills. If you can dig holes and move a wheelbarrow, you have a good start. Depending upon the projects you want to tackle, you might also need some basic carpentry, masonry, and plumbing skills.

If you're not sure how much landscape design skill you have, take heart. There are some specific things, discussed below, you can do to practice and strengthen your skill before you actually begin in your own yard. The more you practice, the better a visionary you will become. If you still feel uncertain, you can always call in some professional help for at least a part of your landscape project. See Chapter 4, "Landscape Professionals," for suggestions on how a pro can help a do-it-yourselfer.

For people in the design phase of landscaping, the first thing I recommend is a good set of tires or shoes. Spend some time driving, bicycling, or walking around the area where you live. Concentrate on neighborhoods where people have lived for a while rather than on new subdivisions. Recently planted landscapes, which may look good on first sight, too often hide design surprises, such as overplanting, that will pop up like a jack-in-the-box in another year or two.

In older areas—places where landscapes have matured for twenty or thirty years or more—it becomes much easier, even for an unpracticed eye, to see which landscape ideas work and which don't. Look for trees that overpower houses or that have heaved up driveways and sidewalks; hedges, shrubs, and groundcovers encroaching where cars or people need access; sagging walls; and general jungle where

Natural Northwest vista: scenic lake and mountains framed by tall firs.

An excellent way to see a variety of well-done landscapes is to go on some organized garden tours. Most of these happen in spring or summer, when the gardens are in their fullest glory. Here's some advice, though: Try to envision what these yards will look like beyond the current bloom, and try to find out how much care each garden takes to stay in decent shape.

If you have time, then don't stop your investigations at the edge of the city or suburb where you live. Get out your camera and take a walk—in the woods, along the beach, across a streambed. A lot of the best Northwest landscaping is inspired by vistas, or small natural settings first seen in the wild nearby. It will help if you have a painter's or photographer's eye for framing pleasing picture compositions, and if you remember where the word "landscape" first came into use—by a group of painters who depicted natural scenery. In the highest sense, when we modify or create landscapes, we are using the earth as our canvas and painting a living, dynamic picture.

The next way to expand your design talent comes from the printed page. Be on the lookout in bookstores and libraries for books and magazines that examine aspects of horticulture or landscaping interesting to you. Two excellent magazines for our part of the country are *Sunset* and *Pacific Horticulture*. Look in them as well for local gardening columns and calendars of upcoming garden tours, garden club meetings, and sales. For design ideas and numerous

there once was a distinct planting plan. Look as well for that curve of a pathway, combination of colors and textures, or placement of plants that pleases your eye. Don't be afraid to borrow ideas from what you see. Take photographs of the landscapes you especially like, and start a list of favorite plants. If you see plants you like but can't identify, take your photos (or take clippings, if you can get permission) to your local nursery or Master Gardener clinic.

advertisements for choice or hard-to-find landscape materials and structures, such as gazebos, pools, and bridges, seek out *Garden Design* and *Landscape Architecture.* I have included my favorite gardening books and magazines in this book's Reading List, but don't limit yourself to those I mention. Read as much as your time and interest will allow.

Color pictures can be an invaluable guide as you decide which flower and foliage colors will work best in your yard. Garden catalogs, if they are expensively produced, have better pictures of various kinds of plants than do some plant books or encyclopedias. The pictures in some of the cheaper catalogs, though, may give only a very approximate indication of flower or leaf color. A commonplace lavender or violet flower might be painted with a bright blue brush by an enthusiastic advertising department.

Check your radio and television listings for local programs dedicated to gardening issues. They are usually scheduled in the weekend daytime hours, when many people's gardening interest is at its highest. These shows often include call-in periods, when you can ask experts questions about specific plant or landscape problems. If you have a public television station in your area, you might enjoy the *Victory Garden* show. The program is very informative, and although it originates on the East Coast, it occasionally does pieces on Western gardening.

CHAPTER TWO

Visualization

Mapping a Design
for Your Yard

*E*ven if you know what kinds of
plants you want to use in your yard,
even if you have some ideas about
other features or structures you would
like, you might feel uncertain about
how to incorporate everything you
want into the garden. Not everyone
can automatically visualize, without a

bit of help, how things will fit together now, and how the landscape will look after a few years of growth have changed it. Some people can look at bare ground and know where the pathways should go; they can see the soil covered with imaginary greenery; they know which branches to prune from existing trees and shrubs to give the best effect. Lots of other people get mental roadblocks when they start to plan their yards. Does this mean they should give up the idea of doing it themselves?

No. There are techniques that anyone can use to help visualize how his or her yard will look when it is finished, and when five or ten years or more have passed. Some of the techniques are old favorites; others are brand-new, high-tech innovations. I'm going to describe several of them, and I encourage you to use whichever method works for you.

The Yard Map

You already know what a road map looks like. It shows highways, back roads, lakes, rivers, mountains, and other important features in an area from a bird's-eye view. Preparing a similar drawing of your yard will help immensely as you begin your design.

Start by measuring the lot's boundaries. Mark the directions of the compass; it's important to know the course of sun and shadow across your property. Draw in the outlines of your house, driveway, and sidewalk. Sketch in any other existing physical fea-

tures of your property that will be permanent unless you decide otherwise, including trees and bushes. Now use arrows to indicate important physical features outside your property that could affect your plans: a beautiful lake or mountain vista, large trees or bushes in neighboring yards that cast shade into yours, a back-yard auto repair shop, a hulking Winnebago. . . . Clearly, you'll want to capture the good views and hide or minimize the bad.

Make sure your drawing is to scale: If you choose a one-tenth scale (1 inch equals 10 feet) and your house is 40 by 50 feet, the house should be 4 by 5 inches on your drawing. Smaller yards can use a larger scale, perhaps 1 inch to 4 feet. Make your drawing large enough so that you can read any details you put in. If you intend to install many different plant materials, use larger paper and a larger scale so that all the details won't look too crammed. You can use blank paper, but drafting paper with a premarked grid will make your work easier. The absolute minimum paper size for your drawing should be 11 by 17 inches; 17 by 24 inches is even better. Try to make your drawing as accurate as possible. Use a long tape measure in the yard itself, rather than pacing the distances. Rental shops carry tape measures that are 100 feet or longer.

TOPOGRAPHY AND CROSS SECTION: Unless you live on level ground, you should also make a sketch, using the same scale as your main drawing, showing the topography—the lay of the land—of your property.

There is a good chance that a topo map was made for your yard back before the house was built

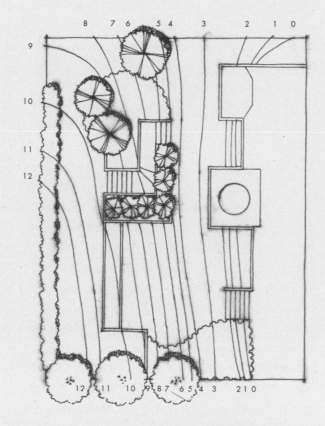

A topo map showing the original grade with a complex railroad-tie wall system superimposed over the topo lines. Zero is the lowest level in the yard, 12 is the highest level; so there is a 12-foot rise from the right to left sides of the picture. Knowing how the land sloped allowed the owner-designer to create three level areas while moving a minimum of soil—and to determine how many ties were needed.

on it. Check the architectural drawings for your house if they are still available. Use the existing topographical map as a starting point, but don't trust it absolutely. I usually find that the earth grading done during and after the house construction has altered the topography some, so a preconstruction elevation map won't be totally on the mark.

If you don't have a topographical map of your yard, or if the one available is not accurate enough, you could hire a surveyor to make one. How precise your map should be depends upon your landscaping needs. If you're going to put in a retaining wall, or if you want to change the grade dramatically or add or remove large volumes of soil, then you need a detailed topo map. It can help you estimate how much material to order or how much you'll need to haul away. If you plan to put any large, permanent structures near your property line, hire a surveyor to make sure that you build only on your own property. I have seen fences, driveways, and even portions of houses fall victim to careless regard for property lines.

If your needs are not very demanding, some cheaper methods could work well enough. You can map the elevation changes in your yard using a length of strong string, two 10-foot poles, and a bubble level. Mark the poles in 6-inch or 12-inch increments so they look like big rulers. Tie one end of the string to each pole, loosely enough to allow you to slip the string up or down on both poles. Hook the

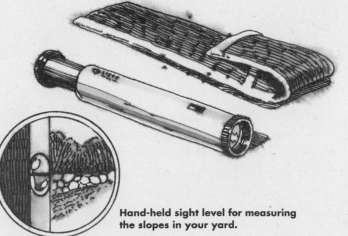

Hand-held sight level for measuring the slopes in your yard.

bubble level to the middle of the string. Choose an area where there is an obvious elevation change, and, with the poles upright, place one pole on the high side, the other on the low. Start with the lowest part of your yard as elevation zero and work up from there. Pull the poles far enough apart to keep the string taut, and slide the string up or down on one pole until the bubble level shows the string is level. Measure the difference between the markings on the high and low poles and then mark each elevation on your yard sketch.

For very long stretches with gradual rises and falls, you might want to use a "pea-shooter" sight level (a kind of hand-held transit) with a marked pole. You can rent one at an equipment rental shop. You can also rent a regular tripod transit, but a pea-shooter is much easier to figure out. You just point the level at the marked pole, sight along the level, raise the far end of the level up or down until the

bubble shows in the middle of your viewer, and then note the difference between the height to your eye level and the height on the marked pole.

For very short distances, you can use a long straight level placed atop a straight board. An 8- or 10-foot two-by-four works fine. Use a tape measure on the downhill side to measure the distance between the board and the ground.

Any of these methods is adequate for simple topographic maps and cross sections. If the area you are designing slopes consistently, then a representative cross section might be all you will need. It is less tedious than doing a complex topographic map.

COMPLETING THE INITIAL DRAWING: Make several copies of your preliminary sketch; you may need all of them to try out different schemes. If your drawing is on 11-by-17-inch paper, then a large-size copier will be sufficient. For sketches on larger paper, you can copy a section at a time using a regular copier, and tape the sections together later—or if you used tracing paper, you can go to a blueprint shop and get blueline or brownline prints. Just make sure that any copies are the same scale as your original, so that you can determine the size of plants and structures with accuracy.

STARTING THE DESIGN: Now you are ready to start planning changes. Using an easily erasable pencil and a good gum eraser, you can begin to

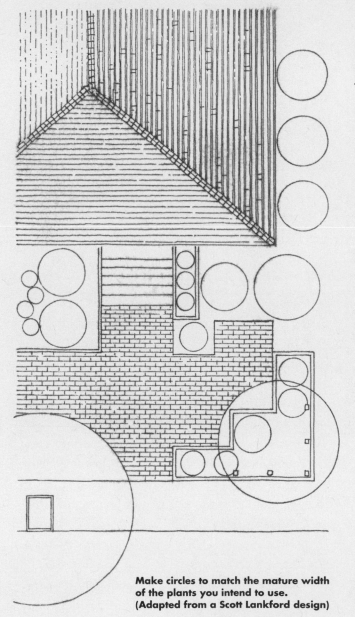

Make circles to match the mature width of the plants you intend to use. (Adapted from a Scott Lankford design)

sketch in any new structures that will be permanent additions to the yard. It's important to begin with these human-specific elements so that you don't box yourself into any design dead ends later. First, determine how foot and wheel traffic will move. Wheel traffic could include a wheelbarrow, wheelchair, lawn mower, boat trailer, or mobile home. Will you need sidewalks? Steps? Driveways? Next, mark in where the permanent structures—fences, sheds, decks, patios, gazebos, and the like—should go. Expect to take some time with this.

After you have done this, start the plant-planning phase. A good way to visualize where things should go is to make cutouts for the various plants and then shift them around on the paper until they make a pleasing pattern. Several companies make landscape design kits with useful transparent cutouts for various sizes and types of trees and shrubs. You can also cut your own, using sheets of different-colored paper. Make large circles for the trees, smaller circles for the plants. Use a good garden encyclopedia if you don't know how large each tree or shrub species will eventually get, and be sure to make the circles to match the scale of your drawing. If you are working with a one-fourth scale drawing (1 inch of drawing equals 4 feet of yard) and are contemplating a tree that will have a spread at maturity of 30 feet, then your circle will need to be 7.5 inches (30 inches divided by 4) across. A circle cut to reflect the plant's mature size will be much more helpful to you than a circle based on the size of the tree when you plant it. If this method prevents you from planting a weeping willow or some other act of botanical terrorism in a small urban courtyard, you will be rewarded many times over in the years to come. This simple circle-making design trick can also help you avoid other plant collisions as the small things you plant grow up and begin to compete for nutrients, water, light—and space.

When you have shuffled the plants and trees around on your drawing until they are placed where you want them, you can either tape the tree and plant circles to the copy of the sketch you are using, or trace around the edges of the circles to transfer your design onto the drawing itself. When you've done that, you can begin to identify on the drawing the names of the plants and trees you want to use.

A NEW PERSPECTIVE: Working with circles on paper helps a lot of people, but it does have one drawback: Everything is shown in two dimensions, from a bird's-eye view. This is a useful tool, but it does not help most people visualize how things will look from the street or from their house. If you have difficulty translating a two-dimensional plan into real life, you might benefit from one or more pictures to show how things will look from a ground-level point of view. Here is a simple way to show things from this new perspective.

Take a series of photographs of your yard. Stand out on the street and take a few snapshots facing

The original photo is blown up on a copier, then a cutout of a mature Japanese maple is superimposed onto the blowup.

toward your house. Stand in the back yard and take some more. Then go inside your house and take shots looking out the main windows. You might also want to take pictures of important features in your yard or nearby which could have an effect on your landscape design, such as desirable or undesirable views or existing trees and structures. Have the best shots blown up to a larger scale. You could simply use an enlarging copier to do this. Make the enlargement 8 by 10 inches or larger so that details show effectively.

A bird's-eye-view sketch shows how wide across things will be, but not how tall they will get.

Now make some cutouts in the shape of the various plants and trees you would like to use. You can draw your own pictures to cut out, or you can copy or trace them from illustrated plant catalogs or books. Use the house itself to give you a sense of the scale you are working with. If your house is 20 feet tall, and it appears to be 6 inches tall on the photo or copy, then a tree with a mature size of 40 feet would require a cutout 12 inches high. Once you have manipulated the cutouts until you have them positioned on the photo where you want them, do as you did with the tree and plant circles on the map-view drawing you made earlier: Tape or transfer the images onto the photo.

You might like to compare this kind of layout with the idealized layout from the bird's-eye-view sketch above. Do they seem to match fairly well? If they don't, you may need to do some rethinking about the parts that don't match. What I often find is that the two kinds of drawings reveal different things about a yard. A two-dimensional drawing shows how wide across things will be, but not how tall they'll get. A perspective montage can show how plants and structures look from a given angle, but may hide details visible from other angles.

There is another way to go beyond two dimensions. You can build a model. I was reminded of this about ten years ago when Ed Mirabella, one of my landscape students, brought to class a scale model of a railroad-tie wall he was thinking of building in his back yard. The miniature wooden structure made a big impression on the class. It also served well as a template for the construction of the actual wall. This is not a new idea, of course. Urban planners and designers of large estates often make scale models of structures and plantings to clarify their intentions to clients and the interested public. It also makes perfect sense for homeowners to do this. Your model doesn't have to be fancy. You could even start with children's nondrying modeling clay, sculpting out land forms as part of a model to guide you when you actually start to grade your yard. If you are more ambitious, you could add forms for trees and shrubs too.

HIGH-TECH DESIGN: If you do any work with personal computers, you are probably aware that all of the visualization techniques I have mentioned so far in this chapter can be done with a computer. And if you are adept with general-purpose CAD (computer-aided design) or paint software, you realize that much of this shuffling around of paper cutouts can instead be done neatly, simply, and quickly with images on a computer screen. You can draw freehand lines and curves, then fill in areas with colors, patterns, or repeated objects—in this case trees, plants, and structures. You can use the software to make either aerial-view or ground-level perspective images of your yard. If you have a 3-D CAD program, you might be able to tilt the image or show it from different perspectives. If you have an image scanner, you can also read images from photographs, drawings, and other printed sources and put them onto the computer's screen, where you can manipulate them. When you have finished creating the image(s) you want, you can save the results on disk for future reference or print your design on a suitable printer.

Some software programs are tailored specifically for landscape design. Some of these are costly, complicated packages meant for professional landscape architects and designers; others are intended more for the home market. You will find more and more of these advertised on the pages of garden magazines as time passes. You can find these through just about any software vendor.

If you have a talent for manipulating images on a computer screen, using a computer to help you visualize your garden design can be a helpful and entertaining activity; if you shy away from computers or don't have one handy, this approach can be intimidating. Keep in mind your level of interest. If you are comfortable with computers, I would encourage you to use one for landscape planning. Otherwise, try the old-fashioned cut-and-paste approach. Either way, I think you will like the results.

Seeing the Steps along the Path

When you begin to put images—of your yard and house, of living and nonliving objects—down on paper, you will benefit if you already have your blue-sky list from Chapter 1 ready. Use your notes on what you do and don't like about other yards, and apply what you have been learning to your own yard.

Coloring in your cutouts can help you determine whether your color choices go well together, and a color wheel can help you choose complementary hues. If you are still not sure how certain color combinations look together, you might want to consider planting a high percentage of annuals for the first year or two. If you decide after seeing certain colors together in your garden that the combinations work, you can either repeat the plantings in future years, or substitute more permanent shrubs and perennials with the same colors. If the combinations don't work, you can begin again fairly inexpensively the next year. Keep a record of good and bad combinations.

I personally think it is more fun, and makes for a more interesting garden, if there are a few near-color-collisions or a few hints of chaos rather than having absolutely everything in place. Even in some of the strictly formal gardens of Spain, where the hedges and shrubs have been tailored into submission to geometric ideals, you will see the orderliness leavened with the uncontainable exuberance of bougainvillea. In the midst of regularity, there hides a romantic heart. The balance between orderliness and verve in your garden depends upon your personal style. We will discuss more about the role style plays in landscaping in the pages to come.

Avoiding Obstacles

There are two roadblocks to landscaping: the obstacles you can see, and those you can't. Some of the obstacles are right there in your yard, while others exist only on paper. It's really not difficult to deal with them. They cause problems only if you ignore them.

UTILITIES: One of the first things I like to do when making a rough sketch of a yard is to draw in where the utilities are. Some of them are aboveground and easy to see; others are belowground, lurking like sharks for the unwary shovel. When I'm not precisely sure where the underground utilities are—which means any time I didn't actually see them go into the ground—I call on the appropriate underground utility location service before I do any digging. In most urban areas, it's a free and convenient service; the number is in the front of the telephone book. The location service can send out a worker to find the hidden utilities within forty-eight hours after you call. Considering how long the landscaping will last once it's in place, two days is not a long time to wait to prevent a great deal of heartache.

Common underground utilities might include:
◆ Power
◆ Phone
◆ Cable TV
◆ Gas
◆ Water
◆ Sewer

Other buried elements might include:
◆ Septic tank and drain field, if you live in an area without sewers;
◆ Yard irrigation systems, including pipes, valves, and wiring;
◆ Landscape lighting systems (these usually have the virtue of at least being low-voltage);
◆ Water drainage systems, consisting of 4-inch corrugated plastic pipe.

Please remember that utility location services have limits as to what they are supposed to find. Ask them what they can and cannot locate. If you have a septic system, for instance, the location services have no means of finding it for you. However, you are likely to find a map of it with the legal papers for your property, or on file with your city or county building-inspection department. Or, you can contact a professional underground utility location service to find those utilities not located by the free service.

There are three good reasons to find out where all these hidden utilities are before you start your yard plan:

- It can cost you an awful lot of money to fix them when you dig them up by mistake.
- It can be extremely unhealthy to cut into some of them. Natural gas and electricity are obvious examples, but digging into sewer, septic, or water systems can also be hazardous to health. Puncturing sewer or septic lines can be a more insidious threat: If you don't realize you've cut into them, you could end up with a hidden leak.
- What you plant near utilities now can cause problems later. Would you plant a weeping willow (*Salix babylonica*) or a row of Lombardy poplars (*Populus nigra* 'Italica') near water- or sewage-bearing pipes if you knew what those trees would do to the pipes? Can you afford to fix the damage they will eventually cause?

Don't forget overhead utilities, either. Phone, power, and cable TV lines may be aboveground in your area. Anything you plant beneath these lines runs the risk of growing up through them and making your life complicated, both financially and aesthetically. Frequently you'll find you can change the intended location of your tree or trees rather than plant directly under wires—and certainly the easiest time to move trees is while they are still on the drawing board. If you can't do that, try either to use trees that will not grow tall enough to threaten the wires or to choose species that are amenable to pruning.

RESTRICTIVE COVENANTS: Depending on the area where you live, you may have restrictive covenants attached to the property you own. They might govern whether or where you can store a boat or a recreational vehicle on your property. They might govern how high a fence you can build, or what its design may be, or whether you can build a storage shed, a pool, or some other structure on your property. There might be provisions limiting tree height so that no views will be blocked—and trees can grow into the bitterest disputes. You might find covenants running with the property that you don't like or that have no current legal standing. If you have questions about any of the provisions, it's time to consult a lawyer.

Locating the hidden utilities in your yard can save you money, prevent health hazards, and tell you where and what to plant.

EASEMENTS: The legal papers regarding the purchase of your property should also say whether or not there are any easements on your land. These could be roadway, sewer, or water easements or the like. Easements give authorities the right to gain access to those portions of land under easement to do any maintenance or construction work that might be required. This might not mean you can't improve the area by putting in plants or lawn, but you should realize that such plantings may be temporary. Don't plant anything of special value that can't stand an unscheduled transplant. And don't put any permanent structures or improvements on land encumbered with easements.

PERMITS: Some cities and counties require that homeowners get permits before doing certain projects in their yards. These projects could include:

- Retaining walls. If you intend to build a wall over 30 inches high, check with your local construction or building department. They might ask you to produce a report from a soils engineer showing that the underlying soil will adequately support the wall. They might also ask for a construction plan showing how you intend to build the wall and what materials you want to use.
- Raised decks or other structures.
- Irrigation systems or outdoor plumbing for hot tubs, spas, and pools. Poorly designed watering systems can cause pollution problems in the water supply;

they also can waste a major amount of water.

- Electrical systems. Low-voltage lighting and sprinkler valve wiring are relatively safe, but anything with household current deserves an inspection. I consider myself lucky to be alive after one meeting with some amateurish underground wiring, and I know of others who were not as lucky.
- Major soil movement. Some areas require permits if you have more than 50 cubic yards of soil added to, removed from, or shifted about on your property. Check with your local land-use department to see what restrictions there are. They might have concerns about adding large masses of loose soil onto potentially unstable hillside lots or filling in low, wet areas. What might look to you at first like a useless swamp could seem a wildlife habitat to others.

A Word about Neighborly Relations

There is a moment in the legend of Pecos Bill when his mother discovers that new neighbors have moved in just forty miles away. This so disgusts her that she drags her family farther out west. Today our neighbors are more likely to be 40 feet away, and our TV goes haywire whenever the neighbors turn on their microwave—yet we're likely to know more about what's happening in the Middle East than in our neighborhood. As lot sizes get smaller, good neighborly relations become increasingly important.

On a simple level, this can mean something as basic as not planting tall-growing trees or hedges that will shade your neighbors' vegetable patch. It could also mean talking with your neighbors about appropriate fence styles, or working to harmonize planting beds, shrubs, and trees in one yard with those next door. Your landscaping doesn't have to copy your neighbor's landscaping, but it doesn't need to clash, either. There are few things more useless than warring landscapes, with the McClouds pitting their Douglas firs against the Franklins' Norway maples, or the Coronas' alpine meadow battling the Smiths' desert scene.

On a more profound scale, whatever we do on our land has an effect far beyond the boundaries of our property. Some people take pride in being stewards to the natural wonders in their yard—the plants, trees, and wildlife living there—while others enjoy the challenge of creating something totally new, personalized to their tastes. Both approaches to landscaping can be responsible, and either one is superior to utter indifference.

CHAPTER THREE

Taking Stock

Evaluating the
Yard You Have

Sometimes it's simpler to start with
nothing at all in the yard; then we
don't have to decide the merits of
existing features. But not all of us buy
houses like that. Older houses will
have established landscaping—mature
plants and trees, existing walkways,
fences, patios, and other structures.

Even with new houses, the developer might have left tall trees in place, or planted new shrubs and trees and installed a sod lawn in order to help sell the house. This kind of landscaping can be a mixed blessing, depending upon whether the existing trees have escaped hidden damage and the installation was properly done. Sometimes the landscaping needs no changes at all—it already meets your needs and taste perfectly. But more often things need some adjustment. In this chapter, we'll cover the basic guidelines to help you decide what, if anything, needs to change. The rules are the same, incidentally, whether you're looking at a house and yard you've just bought, or at your present lot with renewed interest. You will have to decide whether what's already there should be kept, moved, or cut.

When you put down earnest money to buy your house, perhaps you wrote a contingency clause into the agreement stating that you agreed to purchase the house contingent upon your acceptance of an inspector's report. The inspector went through the house, checking the condition of the foundation, drainage, plumbing and electrical systems, the mortar in the chimney, the roof—the list goes on. Perhaps he or she also gave you some pointers on the condition and safety of various yard structures, such as fences and patios.

But what about an inspector for the landscaping—someone who checks out the condition of the soil, appropriateness and condition of the plantings, potential problems with pests, pruning, and watering? Sometimes a former owner's faulty planning or poor maintenance can cost you more in the yard than the repairs to the house. I suggest that you do a yard inspection, either before you buy or after, so that you can be on the alert for potential problems and deal with them before they become even more costly. You can do this inspection either by yourself or in cooperation with an outside expert, perhaps a landscape architect or designer, or landscape contractor. If you're not sure, after reading this chapter, how to proceed, see Chapter 4, "Landscape Professionals," for descriptions of different types of landscape experts who could be useful.

Taking an Inventory

The first step in analyzing the landscaping in your yard is to take inventory of your existing plants: what they are, what condition they are in, how well they are positioned, and what problems and advantages they present.

IDENTIFICATION: If you are new at plant identification, there are some inexpensive sources of help. You can always take clippings (or well-focused, properly lighted photographs) of the various plants in your yard to your local nursery. Flowers, leaves, berries, and seedpods all help. Unless you go on a busy weekend or a sunny spring day, you are likely to find someone with the time to tell you what plants you have and which are worth keeping. You will also find the local Master Gardener clinics helpful.

Taking this inventory will prevent what happened at one house I know. The new residents, in an effort to tidy up the yard, tore out hundreds of dollars' worth of perennials and groundcovers, and prepared to haul everything to the dump. Alert neighbors rushed over and begged for some of the gleanings, which benefited everyone—the haul to the dump cost much less because so much of the debris ended up thriving in neighboring yards. The simple act of identifying plant material could be an enriching experience. If you have plant material in your yard that you don't like (and you are not obligated to like it) but that has some value to others, you might be able to sell or trade some of it to your local nursery for plants more suited to your tastes and needs—or you might be persuaded to give some of the material a chance, since appreciation often comes with knowledge. If there are plants you dislike and no longer want in your yard, invite your friends and neighbors to dig out what you don't want.

I don't recommend that people pop their least-favorite plants out of the ground and then drag them around to all the nearby nurseries. Some nurseries

If you have plant material that you don't like, you might be able to sell or trade some of it.

won't consider trades or purchases from noncommercial sources. If a nursery is interested in the plants in your yard, it may prefer to send a crew out to dig things in the proper digging season. Have no doubt that a nursery will be interested only in those plants which are easiest to transplant or which have a great value relative to their size. This could include rare or large rhododendrons and their relatives, special conifers, rare bulbs, Japanese maples (*Acer palmatum* cv.), or perennials. It absolutely will not include common junipers (*Juniperus* spp.), undernourished, diseased, disfigured, or bug-ridden plants, or anything that the nursery could get with less effort or cost from one of its regular commercial growers.

CONDITION: The better a plant looks, the more likely it is you will want to keep it. If some of the plants in your yard are in less than ideal condition, you will be better able to make a wise decision about their future if you know what has gone wrong. A plant may suffer because of poor soil preparation, poor placement, or poor care.

It is usually easy to tell if a plant has been attacked by enemies. Holes chewed in leaves or in trunks are a sure sign of insect assault. You might also see insects directly on the leaves. Plant diseases may be harder to diagnose, but look for dead branches, or discoloration or growths on branches or leaves. Sometimes dead branches are a sign of winter damage, caused by too much cold or wind-induced drying of foliage, followed by secondary bacterial or fungal infections. If you aren't sure why a plant doesn't look good, you can get in-person help by taking a fresh clipping from it to a Master Gardener clinic or to your local nursery. Be sure to call the nursery first to see if the owners mind having diseased or bug-ridden leaves brought onto their land.

Animals sometimes damage plants as well. Although rhododendrons are poisonous, I know of one back yard full of decapitated rhodies, destroyed by a bored but still-healthy Labrador retriever. Cats can kill plants by converting them to scratching posts. In more remote areas, deer, mountain beavers, and other wildlife may cause damage by foraging for food.

Plants can be smothered by the gradual buildup of bark mulch around their roots; this is especially common in yards where a few inches of bark mulch are added every year or so to refresh the look of the mulch. Carefully scrape away a small section of mulch about a foot away from the base of a suspect plant to see how deeply the mulch has piled up. There should be no more than an inch or so of bark mulch covering the roots; more than that can be more harmful than none at all. Buried plants will benefit either from careful removal of some of the mulch over the roots or by being lifted and replanted higher in the soil. Examine the soil underneath as you replant. You may find that poor soil is contributing to the problem too. See Chapter 8, "Site Preparation,"

for help in determining the quality of your soil.

You don't have much control over how plants in your yard were treated before you arrived. Homeowners often go into a frenzy of yard activity just before they put their house on the market, trying to make up for years of neglect. Sometimes they do superficial weeding, leaving the roots intact and covering up the evidence with a layer of fresh bark mulch. Sometimes sellers will assault the shrubbery with whatever pruning tools are at hand, with an eye more to expediency than to the future health or shape of the plants.

Pruning errors are usually the easiest to spot. Look for decapitated plants or trees, with stubs of branches or limbs unadorned by foliage. Unless you are fond of very formal garden design, beware of yards in which everything, regardless of species, has been pruned into spheres, mounds, or cubes. Although some plants tolerate continual, close pruning, others are damaged by it. If a pruning job has been botched, you will have to decide whether a particular plant can recover or whether it's a hopeless cause.

Weeds are a more insidious challenge. They are especially frustrating to handle when they infest rockeries with plants in the crannies, or stands of groundcovers. If the weeds are particularly difficult—horsetail, morning glory (field bindweed), and some grasses come to mind—it's usually easier to rip out weeds and groundcovers alike and start over than it is to try pulling out just the weeds and their roots. (You do have to get the weed roots out, too, or the weeds will pop back quickly and you'll be faced with the same task again.) If you are patient, you can take cuttings from the plants you tear out to help you start over. My sympathies are with you if you should discover horsetail in your yard. You might want to consider moving.

Although there are some chemicals designed to suppress weed development in established plant beds, I am not enthusiastic about them. They must be used with great care and only with the plants listed on the label. Dichlobenil, the active ingredient in the most famous pre-emergent weed killer, cannot be used in areas with perennials or annuals or in any place where you hope to change the plantings from time to time. Be especially careful of runoff to lawn areas or planting beds with vulnerable plants.

POSITION: Every plant requires a certain amount of room to thrive. Because so many landscapes are overplanted, you may find plants in your yard that are competing for a limited amount of space. Some of the plants will be losers. Look for plants that lean out away from the house; look for dead branches on a plant's shadiest side, where the plant has given up; look as well for branches of different plants interlacing in a chaotic struggle. These are all signs that the plants were planted too close to each other or to the house. This does not necessarily mean that one or more of the plants should be removed. Sometimes carefully trimming back conflicting branches can help. Sometimes thinning out the front branches will make a plant look better balanced and will allow sufficient light into the shadier spots. Pruning like this will help you avoid the gap-toothed effect that happens when a mature plant is removed from a group.

If your efforts do leave a visible gap in the landscape, you might be able to rearrange the nearby branches of the surviving plants or trees to help fill in by tying them over into the vacant space. Leave them tied for at least one growing season and then remove the ties so that the branches do not get damaged as they grow.

Plants also suffer if they are planted in inconvenient locations. One of my favorite examples of this is a Colorado blue spruce (*Picea pungens* 'Glauca') that was planted where a walkway meets a driveway. Its striking blue foliage looked attractive for about three years, but Colorado spruce is the northern-climate equivalent of cactus. When its needle-sharp foliage started poking out at passers-by and car paint, the homeowners began to prune back the branches. Spruces don't recover well from this kind of aggressive pruning; the tree gradually lost its graceful symmetry and became spectacularly ugly. I suppose the owners left it in place in spite of its ugliness because they remembered how expensive it was originally. Unfortunately, unlike other costly but unattractive possessions, outdoor plants can't very well be hidden in a dark spot in the garage, so we continue to display them publicly.

Plants and trees can pose obstacles of other sorts too. If you find yourself not using a walkway because plants cover or block it, it might be time to move the plants. If the plants are very large, in good shape, and otherwise well placed, it could be better—and cheaper—to move the walkway.

When plants have grown up and covered windows, cutting off the entry of sunlight into a house, it no longer matters whether the plants are well shaped. Windows are designed to let in sunlight and let people look out at the scenery. There is also the issue

Pfitzer junipers engulfing a gate. Planted as groundcovers, they grow more like horizontal trees, and are a poor choice for close quarters.

of security. If your neighbors can't keep an eye on your house because some of its entryways are hidden beneath mounds of foliage, or if you feel uncomfortable walking up to your front porch at night because you don't know what's in the surrounding bushes, then it's time to prune.

VOLUNTEERS: A volunteer is a plant that sprouts and grows even though people didn't plant it. Sometimes volunteers make welcome additions to the garden, but more often they are unwanted intruders, disrupting the planned pattern. If these botanical gate-crashers are low-growing, we are likely to call them weeds and deal with them as such. But if the volunteers are trees or identifiable shrubs, we are more likely to let them grow, even if they are in awkward, inappropriate places. Although we wouldn't think of planting an alder (*Alnus rubra*), a bigleaf maple (*Acer macrophyllum*), or a Western red cedar (*Thuja plicata*) into the side of a rockery on purpose, would we cut it down if it sprouted there? Other native trees are likely to pop up in your yard too—various species of false cypress (*Chamaecyparis* spp.), different pines, Western hemlock (*Tsuga heterophylla*), and Douglas fir (*Pseudotsuga Menziesii*). Maybe we are reluctant to cut down volunteer trees because most of them make fine landscape trees if they are planted in the right spot. (For alder and bigleaf maple, the right spot is in a very large woodland setting, not a small urban lot.)

Trees are not the only intruders. Perhaps you have a stray cotoneaster growing in an odd spot. They sprout readily from seed carried everywhere by birds, which eat the bright red berries. If you want to create a wintertime food source for birds, then you might want to move the cotoneaster to a more appropriate spot. Or perhaps you have forget-me-nots popping up everywhere. Do you keep them because they are pretty? Or do you tear them out because they are choking out other equally valuable plants? If you don't decide, the plants will decide for you.

TREES: Trees can be troublemakers even if they aren't volunteers. It's important to evaluate trees planted by design too, because they form the backbone of your landscape. Don't assume that a tree is harmless just because it has not yet caused obvious harm. If the tree is alive, it is likely to continue growing, and with each new twig it can become more of a maintenance burden. I sometimes drive down tree-lined boulevards with a sense of wonder. I wonder, when the planning department decided to plant street trees under power lines, whether it considered where the money would come from to pay for the maintenance of those trees. If you have trees growing beneath wires in your yard, look carefully at their shapes. Have they been top-trimmed to keep them out of the wires? That means that the chore of maintenance has already begun. Has the trimming been done in an aesthetic manner, so that the shapes are

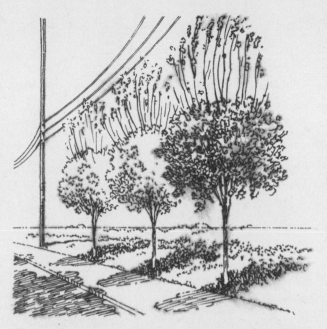

These Norway maples will require constant pruning to keep them out of the power lines, and they'll *never* look good.

still pleasing, or are the trees merely crew-cut? Although utility departments may foot the pruning bills for trees on public rights-of-way, you are likely to be responsible for those growing under the lines serving your house, and you might not like the results of utilitarian pruning.

Now step inside the house and look out each of the windows in turn. If some of your trees block off views of lakes, mountains, or other valuable visual real estate, you'll have to decide which you prefer, the tree or the view. You might be able to prune the tree to keep it from blocking the view, but that depends on what kind of tree it is. Slow-growing trees or trees with strong horizontal branching patterns may be suitable for planting beneath utility lines or scenic vistas. These could include dwarf or semidwarf apple or plum trees, or certain ornamental flowering trees, including the wide-spreading flowering cherries (*Prunus* spp.), pink dogwood (*Cornus florida* 'Rubra'), or kousa dogwood (*Cornus kousa*). These trees are likely to be worth the effort of occasional pruning, if it is ever needed. Less suitable would be most pear and fruiting cherry trees, because of their more upright growth habit, and most evergreen trees, which grow too fast and don't look good when topped. Other bad choices for planting under wires are birch (*Betula* spp.), most maples (*Acer* spp.), oak (*Quercus* spp.), and most other large shade trees.

Trees planted too near human structures pose problems too. If a tree is shallow-rooted, or if it is planted on poor soil, it will likely heave up and break any nearby driveways or walkways. Any of the faster-growing trees above can cause problems, but be especially wary of trees like weeping willow (*Salix babylonica*), bigleaf maple (*Acer macrophyllum*), London plane tree (*Platanus acerifolia*), poplar (*Populus* spp.), and locust (*Robinia* and *Gleditsia* spp.). Watch for roots right at the surface, snaking out across lawns and under pavement. The upheaval is both unsightly and dangerous for pedestrians.

Trees near houses can crack concrete foundations and walls; they can ineluctably push apart rock-

eries; their shade and leaf-drop can encourage moss and accelerate deterioration of roofs. Of course, more than leaves can drop when storm winds hit the region. A few trees are sometimes acceptable for planting very near houses. Several of the upright cultivars of Japanese maple (*Acer palmatum* cv.), our native vine maple (*Acer circinatum*), strawberry tree (*Arbutus unedo*), sourwood (*Oxydendron arboreum*), the weeping crabapples (*Malus* spp.), and some of the dwarfer or weeping pines can be used effectively near a windowless stretch of house siding—as little as 5 to 7 feet from the foundation. Beware of bigger trees, though. One memorable sound of my childhood was the cannon-shot shudder of Douglas fir branches, 6 to 8 inches in diameter and up to 20 feet long, breaking off and hitting the roof of our family's house. With twin trees, both over 70 feet, poised just outside the house, we were reluctant to spend much time upstairs when the winds howled. Douglas firs, Deodar cedars (*Cedrus deodara*), and most other trees that grow to majestic size should be planted at least 30 feet away from the house. If 30 feet puts it in someone else's yard, good. Consider getting it out of your yard.

One favorite trick of large-tract developers is to clear-cut most of the trees in a development, leaving only a few gangly, exposed specimens. Such trees are

◆

If some of your trees block off scenic views, you'll have to decide which you prefer—the tree or the view.

◆

at special risk for two reasons: they lack the protection from wind that trees can get when growing in groups; and the earth-moving activity upsets the soil structure supporting the few remaining trees, making them more vulnerable to toppling. Other environmental damage can include the cutting of vital tree roots by backhoes or bulldozers, or simply the compaction of soil over tree roots by the repeated passage of heavy equipment. Either cutting or compaction can be enough to kill the trees. This is why many landscapers place bets on how long a given stand of trees will survive the encroachment of civilization: Will the trees live until all the lots in the development have sold? Will they linger for a few months or years of dwindling splendor before expiring? Our native big-leaf maple and Western red cedar are two of the most fragile trees in this respect, surpassed only by the beautiful but extremely touchy madrona (*Arbutus Menziesii*).

My wife and I decided to keep our red cedars for aesthetic and environmental reasons, including the trees' contribution to air quality.

If you decide that some of the trees planted in your yard are in the wrong place, you might want to either take them down or (if they are small enough) move them. Certainly, most trees under 6 to 8 feet tall present no great challenge to move; with larger trees you will reach a point where the effort involved in moving them is likely to outweigh the cost of buying replacements. Read Chapter 10, "Planting and Transplanting," for some suggestions on when and how to move trees.

When poorly sited trees present too big a challenge to move, I have no major objection to cutting them down. Don't move too quickly, though. My wife and I made the choice at our new house not to cut down several enormous Western red cedars. Even though they create enough shade in the yard to hinder our vegetables and roses and they lay a new covering of debris on the roof after each storm, we balanced aesthetic and environmental concerns, including the trees' contribution to air quality, and decided to give the red cedars a reprieve. Some messy bigleaf maple trees did lose out though. We also decided to install two new view windows, each facing a special vista out into the yard and the horizon beyond. The increased light and views from the new windows offset the hulking shade of the Western red cedars, and we discovered that the trees protect our house from the worst of the summer heat. If we had cut them down when we first moved in, we would never have known that. The red cedars will stay.

Beyond Plants

This is a good time to take stock of the structures in your yard too. Examine your walkways, decks, gazebos, patios, and fences with a critical eye. Ask yourself two questions about each one: Is it in good condition? And is it appropriate? The second question is more important. If something doesn't suit your needs, then it doesn't matter how good it looks. A family in our neighborhood filled in their swimming pool last summer and turned the site into a sport court, complete with basketball hoop and tennis net. Do they swim? Yes, in a public pool a few blocks away. But now they don't have to worry as much about where their children are playing—or where the neighborhood children play when they themselves are away—and they pay far less in pool fees than they did in liability insurance, pool chemicals, and heating costs. Simply put, they looked at their yard with a critical eye, and then they bought some peace of mind.

On a smaller scale, I did the same thing eight years ago when I filled in with soil a small fish pond I had built in our yard. The pond looked fine, but it lost its charm when a three-year-old visitor plopped headfirst into it. Caution won out, and the pond had to go.

Use this same kind of critical process on the other structures in your yard. One of the fads of the 1960s was to put up sheet-metal tool sheds. A big disadvantage of most of these units is that they dent. If your shed looks like a partly crushed pop can, it might be time to recycle it. Or perhaps you have the hulk of a greenhouse off in a corner. Are its structure and foundation sound enough to merit a fix-up? And would you use it if it were in good condition? About half of the home greenhouses I see are ignored by their owners. Rather than exhort people to take advantage of an inherited greenhouse, I am more inclined to simply say: use it or get rid of it.

Next take a look at any fences in your yard. Check the posts right at the ground. If they are rotting away, it would be good to replace them with pressure-treated posts. Although I can understand why people may be reluctant to use chemically treated wood to make raised beds for vegetable gardens, I think it's worthwhile to use treated wood for fence posts. Maybe that's because I see too many fences blown over by winter storms. Several companies now make pressure-treated fence boards too, but even untreated fence boards should last a long time— if they don't touch the ground. If soil or bark mulch is sloughing against your fence boards, it's time to raise the bottom of the fence or pull away the material touching it.

CHAPTER FOUR

Landscape Professionals

How a Pro Can Help the Do-It-Yourselfer

*I*t may seem strange to devote a chapter of a do-it-yourself book to landscape architects, landscape designers, landscape contractors and gardeners, and nursery staff. Yet each kind of landscape professional fills a particular niche, and one or more of them could prove helpful to your do-it-yourself landscape plans. I'll start out with the most expensive type of expert and work my way down.

Landscape Architects

Not everyone who designs landscapes is a landscape architect. A landscape architect must first earn a bachelor's or master's degree in landscape architecture from a qualified college or university, leaving school with training in the design of both public and private spaces—parks, cityscapes, highway plantings, boulevards, and both grand and humble home landscapes. He or she then typically works in the office of an established landscape architect for a length of time and then must pass a state accreditation test before becoming licensed.

Many people are intimidated when they hear the word "architect." Sometimes they have a right to be. A landscape architect may well be the most expensive kind of professional, on an hour-by-hour basis, of any you will read about in this chapter. He or she could also be one of your best investments.

A rule of thumb that some landscape architects use is that, ideally, homeowners should spend about 10 percent of the cost of their house and property on the landscaping—plants, trees, soil, other materials, labor, and design. A $100,000 house, then, should have about $10,000 worth of landscaping; a $300,000 house should have about $30,000 worth. This might not sit very well with you if you have already stretched your budget to move into your dream house. What you decide to do depends partly upon your budget and partly upon your level of interest. If it is important to you to have a well-executed design for your yard, then consider getting help from a landscape architect.

Not everyone needs—or can afford—a landscape architect's full range of services. Some landscape architects will do a one- or two-hour consultation, pointing out how to take advantage of existing features in your yard and how to avoid potential problems. This could be enough to get you started in the right direction, especially if you organize your thoughts beforehand. Following the steps in Chapter 1, "Chasing a Vision," would be a good preliminary, whether you need a little help or a lot.

If you want a well-executed yard design, consider hiring a landscape architect.

Some landscape architects are also willing, for a fee, to visit your site at various stages of the landscaping process to check on the work in progress. This is standard practice when you hire a landscape architect for extensive services, but it may also be possible on an occasional or as-needed basis.

Landscape Designers

Many of the comments about landscape architects also hold true for landscape designers. What is

MAKE SURE THAT any landscape professional you choose—whether landscape architect, designer, contractor, or otherwise—is attuned to your particular tastes and needs. Here are a few guidelines:

- Make sure you communicate what your overall budget will be. It won't do you much good to get limousine plans if you have a bicycle budget.

- Try to verbalize your personal style. I've seen a number of wonderful plans stay on paper because of miscommunication. And whose fault is it? The designer should listen to your needs and draw them out, in both senses of the phrase; but you must also be able to express those needs clearly and firmly. After all, you're the one who will be living with your garden. Share with your professional any homework you have done already concerning your needs. If you've done some preliminary sketches, bring those out too. No matter how primitive the sketches may look to you, they can give added guidance to the professional.

- Ask to see examples of the landscape professional's work. Sketches are not always helpful—to an untrained eye, all sorts of designs may look good on paper. Ask for photographs, or better yet, addresses. Look critically at designs that have been in the ground for a number of years to see how they've held up.

- If you intend to hire the landscape professional for more than just a one- or two-hour consultation, get references, and talk to the references.

- Ask the professional about his or her philosophy. Some believe in "heritage" landscaping—that is, permanent landscaping that will stay in scale for decades to come; others view landscaping as exterior decorating—something to change when you get bored with it, as you might with wallpaper in the kitchen. Both are legitimate philosophies of landscaping, but don't underestimate the differences between them.

- If you want low-maintenance landscaping, make sure that both you and the designer or landscape architect mean the same thing by that phrase. Are you willing to do occasional sprayings for insects and diseases, or would you prefer not to have plants that will suffer without such care? How much pruning are you able, willing, and skilled enough to do?

- Be sure to tell the landscape architect, designer, or contractor whether you prefer to work with readily available, more affordable materials, or whether you might enjoy some rarer materials that might cost more but may give your yard a distinctive touch. In the latter case, make sure the landscape architect has some sources in mind before he or she makes those recommendations. Just ask: "Where do I find these things?" Few activities are more frustrating for the homeowner or landscape contractor than trying to locate some botanical wonder more elusive than the Holy Grail.

- When a professional suggests that you install an irrigation system, don't automatically tune out. Especially in the first few years after planting, even drought-resistant plantings are likely to need supplementary watering, and few people have the time necessary to do hand-watering satisfactorily.

the difference between the two professions? A landscape designer may or may not have formal training. Some community colleges offer courses or programs in landscape design, often taught by landscape architects. But no degree or apprenticeship is required before someone can adopt the title of landscape designer. Typically, landscape designers will charge less per hour or per job than landscape architects—but the more popular landscape designers in a given area may charge as much as some landscape architects. As a group, landscape architects are likely to focus more on designing the "hardscape"—the structures on and flow of the land—while landscape designers might stress the blending of different plants and materials together into a coherent plantscape.

Many designers specialize in particular types of gardens. They may champion edible landscapes, or cottage gardens, or native habitats, rather than trying to be experts at every kind of landscaping. Look for clues in their advertisements and portfolios—or ask them directly if they prefer to work in a particular style.

Landscape Contractors and Landscape Gardeners

Perhaps you want to do all the development work in your yard; if you have the strength, the time, and the skills, I won't say a word. But what if you want to build a brick wall, or pour an exposed aggregate patio, or put in a rockery, or build a deck? Are you a mason? A concrete finisher? A combination jigsaw-puzzler/weightlifter? A carpenter? This is where an honest "skills inventory" (see Chapter 1) can be useful.

What is the difference between a landscape contractor and a landscape gardener? Sometimes the difference is only in the name; sometimes it is much greater than that. The landscape contractor, who concentrates on the design and installation of landscapes, is required by law to be licensed (typically he or she has a specialty contractor's license, rather than a general contractor's license) and bonded. This protects the homeowner in the event that plants die or something vital springs a leak; it also helps contractors in the collection of their fees.

In the real world, you are likely to find some blurring of the lines between landscape contracting and gardening services.

Many landscape contractors also participate in optional training, such as the state Certified Landscaper programs in Washington and Oregon, which can help to increase their skills and thus make their services more valuable to you. These programs are created in conjunction with the state Certified Nurseryman programs discussed later in this chapter; they include the bulk of the nursery-related programs, but go much further into landscaping specifics.

Landscape gardeners are required to have a business license, but not all have a contractor's license as well. Those that do are called landscape maintenance contractors. Rather than focusing on the construction side of landscaping, many landscape gardeners specialize in keeping already-installed landscaping presentable. They mow and edge lawns, pull weeds, and rake leaves.

Whenever you purchase services, draw up a contract detailing each side's responsibilities.

In the real world, of course, you are likely to find some blurring of the lines between landscape contracting and gardening services. Some landscaping firms do both installation and upkeep, and some maintenance firms do minor landscaping tasks, such as planting seasonal flower beds and occasionally trimming shrubs. Just remember that there are limits to the landscaping knowledge and skills of some of the more casual "mow, blow, and go" crews. If you need help with pruning, look for companies that specialize in that. And if your needs go higher, into tree pruning or removal, then it's time to call in a tree service. It is particularly important that the service be licensed and bonded. For trees of great merit or visibility needing expert care in pruning, look for a tree service with an on-staff arborist or a certified tree surgeon.

Perhaps you know some teenagers or college students in the neighborhood who are willing to help out in your yard with simpler chores, such as weeding, lawn mowing, or wheelbarrowing bark mulch and topsoil. I wouldn't stretch things too much beyond that, however. Although some casual helpers may be skilled enough to do actual landscape construction work, keep in mind that you are likely to be legally responsible in the event of an accident on your property involving an unlicensed contractor.

A last thought about landscape contractors: the key part of the word "contractor" is "contract." Whenever you make a major purchase of services, draw up a contract spelling out in detail the responsibilities of each side. Include the work to be done, the quantity and size of materials to be used, and terms of payment. Before you sign anything, do what you would do with a landscape designer or landscape architect: get references, follow up on them, and examine the quality of work done on previous jobs. Check with the state licensing board to make sure the contractor's license is current. Ask about the professional organizations to which the contractor belongs. And check, too, with the Better Business Bureau in your area.

THE CONTRACTOR AS DESIGNER: Some landscape contractors have their own design staff, or have salespeople who double as landscape designers. This arrangement can improve communication because there is one less layer of business between you and your yard—the design and construction are done by one entity. Sometimes, however, I see pressures working on these in-house design staffs that may affect their recommendations:

- Customers may feel cheated if their landscapes look sparse when completed; they may not feel consoled by the thought that the plants will "grow into" the area. The result: Customers pressure the landscaper to overplant. This is unfortunate, because it sacrifices long-term effectiveness for short-term attractiveness.
- The design/sales staff may be encouraged by management to overplant because more plants mean more profits. The result: The landscaper pressures the customer to overplant.
- Management may encourage the design/sales staff to promote whatever materials are in stock rather than the materials that would best suit your yard. (However, the landscaper might have good reasons for carrying a stock of certain plants, such as their suitability for your area. Don't hesitate to ask ahead of time why the landscaper prefers those materials over others.)
- As with independent landscape architects and designers, it helps if the contractor has experience with the style of landscaping you prefer. Watch out for "one-note" designs—the same design repeated in every yard—especially if they're not in tune with your needs.

Whether you work with an independent landscape architect or designer, or a landscape contrac-
tor's in-house designer, expect to pay for the design time. The designer's stock-in-trade is ideas—creativity blended with knowledge.

Nursery Sales Staff

Although nursery salespeople are there to sell plants and plant supplies, most of them realize that they can sell more plants in the long run by providing accurate answers to your questions and by recommending suitable plants. Both Washington and Oregon have state Certified Nurseryman programs, administered by the state nursery associations, that test nursery salespeople on their knowledge about plants and plant care techniques and products. Certified salespeople have at least a minimum level of competence in their trade; but remember that their training may not have included landscape design.

Because I grew up in a plant nursery environment, I can suggest some pointers on how to get the best information from nursery staffs:

- Don't go on a sunny, crowded weekend when the salespeople are swamped. Visiting on a weekday morning might work out best. Better yet, call ahead and find out when would be the best time to come in with questions.
- Nursery staffs don't charge for supplying information over the counter about appropriate plant choices, but they expect a *quid pro quo* for the time they spend with you.

◆ No single nursery can carry every kind of plant suitable to your area. Most will carry a selection of the popular, more easily grown plants that do well in your area. Some specialize in particular kinds of plants—fruit trees, perennials, rhododendrons, or herbs, for instance. If you have a special plant interest, a specialized nursery is often your best source. But many general nurseries will make an effort to find rare or obscure plant material for you if they don't have it in stock currently.

Other Species of Experts

Depending upon your needs, there are other kinds of experts whom you might want to call in on your landscape project. You could contact a soil-testing service to help you determine the quality of the soil in your yard and what amendments it might require. In some regions, you can use the agricultural extension service (see below); in others, you will have to hire a private firm.

If you are planning a massive retaining wall, you can save a lot of money by consulting a soils engineer. This person will test to see how much load your soil will bear and will recommend materials to use for the wall and backfill. Your county may require that you hire a soils engineer or an equivalent expert for this

advice before granting you a building permit.

◆ ◆ ◆

The one word that sums up this chapter best might be "expertise." If you feel confident in all that you intend to do, you might not need any outside help. But if you're unsure about any phase of your landscaping plan, you might benefit by calling in one or more experts to focus on doubtful areas so you can concentrate on the things you do best.

OTHER RESOURCES: If you're on a tight budget, don't overlook the less-commercial sources of information on landscaping. Your county agricultural extension service is one source, and your Master Gardener program (administered by the argricultural extension service) is another. The agricultural extension service publishes low-cost booklets on numerous landscape-related subjects, and the booklets are strongly written, not like some timid federal publications I have seen. Your public library and local bookstore should be good sources of landscaping and gardening books and magazines. Nearby universities or community colleges often offer informal, noncredit gardening and landscape design classes. In the Reading List, I have included a list of books and magazines on landscaping which I have found helpful and/or enjoyable. I hope you enjoy them too.

CHAPTER FIVE

Maintenance

Planning with Upkeep in Mind

Maintenance is a dirty word. It means you've put a lot of work into your yard, but things won't stay put. Weeds grow, the lawn needs cutting and feeding, the rose bushes are mildewed and black-spotted, and the shrubs and trees cry for attention. Why, you wonder, can't landscaping be like interior decorating? When you do a room, it stays done. Yes, you may have to clean and vacuum, and once in a while you'll have to repaint the walls, but things stay put until you get tired of them and decide to redecorate.

The difference, of course, is that "exterior decorating" involves living things, and living things are by nature dynamic, not static. Furthermore, even the nonliving parts of your yard, such as fences, mulches, and rockeries, are subject to the effects of weather and general wear.

◆

What you put in your yard now will affect how much work you will have to do later.

◆

Since you have a time budget as well as a money budget, let's analyze which landscaping features will demand the most care from you. Why now, before you've started to do anything in your yard? Because what you put into your yard will have a great effect on how much work you will have to do later to keep everything looking good. Preventive maintenance is a good concept, and I support it. But preventive planning should demand your attention too. What follows is a brief overview of some common landscape components from a maintenance viewpoint.

Lawns

Lawns are the top maintenance villains. Given two equal-sized yards, the one with more lawn will require more work. It will require more water, more fertilizer, more labor, and more chemicals (if you use them). A lot of water utilities are promoting smaller lawns as a way to cut down on water consumption. See the Appendix for some groundcover alternatives to lawn; see also the sidebar in Chapter 11, "Lawns."

If you do decide to have some lawn, you can cut down on work, water, and materials if you install it properly; take a look at Chapter 11 for more information.

Plants

Trees, shrubs, and other plantings can take a certain amount of work to keep up as well. But there are some basic guidelines you can follow to minimize your work, all of them centered around one idea—using plants and trees adapted to your yard. Here are the guidelines. We'll discuss each in detail below.

- Put shade-loving plants in the shade and sun-loving plants in the sun.
- Use plants adapted to the kind of soil you have in your yard, or amend your soil to meet their needs.
- Use plants that will stay in scale with your yard.
- Seek out disease- and insect-resistant plant varieties.
- Avoid planting aggressive plants that require lots of pruning to stay neat or that will wreck other plantings in the garden if they are put in the wrong place.

LIGHT: Let's start with the issue of sun and shade.

If a plant needs sun to look its best, what will happen if you plant it in the shade? You'll be letting yourself in for extra pruning and pest-spraying. You'll get fewer flowers. The plant will grow spindly as it tries to find more sunlight. It is also more likely to be subject to mildew and other diseases. For many of you, the best example of this would be the typical hybrid rose. You may get a few flowers from it if it is planted in the shade, but the plant itself is likely to look awful. If you are seriously tempted to plant roses in a shady area, look for roses with hybrid musk parentage; check with your local rose society for additional suggestions. You may want to avoid putting most kinds of conifers in shady areas; this especially includes most spruces (*Picea* spp.) and false cypresses (*Chamaecyparis* spp.). Fans of low-growing junipers whose yards have a fair amount of shade should consider the very hardy juniper relative from Siberia, *Microbiota decussata*.

Shade-loving plants placed in the sun are a problem too. Many conifer cultivars with golden or pale foliage need at least filtered shade or their foliage will burn. You should also avoid putting your prized fuchsia, impatiens, and begonia plantings near a sun-baked sidewalk or driveway. Leaves will burn and flowers will wilt. Even if the plants survive, you won't be happy with the results.

There are even subtler issues at work here. Some plants may be winter-hardy in your area if they are planted where they receive only afternoon sun. This is because they will be less likely to break dormancy too early and start to bud out than plants on the south or east side of your yard. Once a plant breaks dormancy, it is much more vulnerable to damage. Pacific Northwesterners know some of the frustration of not being able to grow certain fruit trees (including most peach, apricot, and almond varieties, and some Japanese plums) with any measure of success—not because the trees aren't hardy, but because they often try to bloom during an early warming spell and then lose their buds during the next mild freeze. Other early-blooming plants, including some camellia varieties, star magnolia (*Magnolia stellata*), and saucer magnolia (*Magnolia* x *Soulangiana*), may suffer as well.

SOIL: How do you determine what kind of soil you have? If you grew up on a farm, there's a good chance you know. But most of us grew up in cities or suburbs, and our only exposure to soils may be from picking some up on the knees of our jeans when we played outside. Take a look at the soil preparation section in Chapter 8, "Site Preparation," for some tips on determining soil content and requirements. Also, when you read plant tags or garden books and catalogs, pay close attention to what they say about soil requirements. Try to limit your choices to those plants that prefer the kind(s) of soils you have or can afford to create.

One reason professional landscapers like to build soil mounds, or berms, in people's yards is to avoid dealing with the inadequacies of the existing soil. Poor drainage, poor aeration, and insufficient organic material are the major villains. By making strategically placed mounds of topsoil, you can raise plant roots so they reside only in decent soil.

SCALE: "Scale" implies that plants should stay in the proper size relationship, both to each other and to the garden in which they grow. If you have an acre or more to landscape, it could make sense to use broad brushstrokes to fill in the design. Your plan might call for using trees that reach majestic size, including some of the so-called "park" trees—deodar and Atlas cedar (*Cedrus deodara* and *atlantica*), Douglas fir (*Pseudotsuga Menziesii*), and sequoia (*Sequoia sempervirens*). Or you could plant an orchard of fruit trees, if you have the time to maintain it and you can use all the fruit.

If you have a smaller garden, it makes sense to use slow-growing plants that will not outgrow the area for many years. Smaller brushstrokes are appropriate here.

Whether your central trees are large or small, accompanying plants should be suited to their scale: Large trees look best with large shrubs, and small trees look best with small shrubs. If you encircled a laceleaf maple with standard-sized rhododendrons, the rhododendrons would soon engulf it. Dwarf rhododendrons or low-growing azaleas would be more appropriate to the maple's petite scale.

If you plant baby giants in a small yard, you will be fighting them forever. If you have a particular favorite plant or tree, find out how large it will be at maturity before you buy it. Often, you will be able to find a perfectly acceptable substitute that will give the same overall effect but won't outgrow its place.

For people who love the shape and growth habit of the weeping willow (*Salix babylonica*) but dislike its greedy roots and extensive spread, I often suggest other weeping trees of a more appropriate scale. For a large garden, this could include weeping beech (*Fagus sylvatica* 'Pendula' and 'Purpurea Pendula') or weeping birch (*Betula pendula* 'Tristis'). They are tall but don't have the massive spread of a weeping willow. Suitable for moderate-sized gardens are Young's weeping birch (*Betula pendula* 'Youngii'), weeping cherry (*Prunus serrulata* 'Pendula' and *Prunus subhirtella* 'Pendula,' among others), weeping crabapples (*Malus* x 'Oekonomierat Echtermeyer' and *Malus* x 'Red Jade,' among others), and weeping katsura tree (*Cercidiphyllum magnificum* 'Pendulum'). For very small gardens, the green- or red-leafed Japanese laceleaf maples (*Acer palmatum* 'Dissectum,' 'Ornatum,' and several others) are ideal. And I haven't even mentioned any of the evergreen weepers available: several weeping junipers, Sargent weeping hemlock (*Tsuga canadensis* 'Pendula'), weeping Norway spruce (*Picea abies* 'Pendula'), Koster weeping blue spruce (*Picea pungens* 'Pendens'), and several weeping pines (*Pinus densiflora* 'Pendula,' *Pinus strobus*

'Pendula,' *Pinus sylvestris* 'Pendula').

I've given plants with weeping branches as one example of plant substitution, but there are countless others that can help you in your specific situation. Perhaps you want a blue conifer but you don't have room for a Colorado blue spruce (*Picea pungens* 'Glauca'). Or perhaps you want a white-flowered rhododendron that won't grow more than three feet high. (Hints: blue-foliaged Skyrocket juniper [*J. virginiana* 'Skyrocket'] and rhododendron 'Dora Amateis.') With the plethora of plants that grow in the Northwest, I feel confident something can be found that will work for your particular yard.

PEST RESISTANCE: It's true. Some plants taste better to bugs than others. Some plants pick up every disease that wafts in with the wind, while others have inborn defenses against outside attack. Knowing this provides you with another useful tool that can cut down dramatically on the time (and money) you spend maintaining your garden. Looking through a vegetable seed catalog, you might notice that some varieties of tomatoes boast of "VFN resistance"; this means that the varieties are less likely to suffer from verticillium, fusarium, and nematode attacks. Certain varieties of other vegetables might offer resistance to other pests. If a particular pest is a problem in your area, I encourage you to plant varieties that can fend off such attacks.

Many other plants have varying levels of pest resistance. Even rose varieties can differ wildly in the amount of care they need. Did you know that some particularly tough roses (including the beautiful, fragrant rugosa roses) are used to help landscape Interstate 90 and other highways and minimal-maintenance parks? It's a good bet they don't get pampered with special fertilizers, watering, or pest control. Look over the potted roses in your local nursery after they have leafed out in late spring or summer. For the moment, ignore the flowers and look at the leaves. Avoid buying those which show the beginnings of the typical rose diseases—mildew, black spot, and rust—even in a nursery environment. Rhododendrons, too, vary in their degree of attractiveness to root weevils: rhododendron 'Elizabeth' and related small red rhododendrons are attractive and frequently damaged, while *R. impeditum, yakusimanum,* 'P.J.M.,' and 'Virginia Richards' will suffer little or no damage. Birches vary in their resistance to the devastating birch-bark borer: Asiatic birches, such as *Betula jacquemontii, B. ermanii,* and *B. platyphylla,* stand up far better to disease than their European and American cousins. The list of resistant plants goes on.

How do you find out which diseases and insects could pose a problem in your area? You can check

> ◆
> *Some plants have inborn defenses against outside attack. By using them, you can reduce the time (and money) spent maintaining your garden.*
> ◆

with your Master Gardener program, or with your agricultural extension service. The Master Gardener clinics can be quite helpful in identifying what is attacking a particular plant of yours.

PRUNING: Some plants always look tidy; if they are planted where they have enough room to grow, they may never need pruning. Others need constant pruning even when given room, just because they have an ungainly growth habit.

Two plants that are on my least-favorite list because of their rampant growth are English laurel (*Prunus laurocerasus*) and English ivy (*Hedera helix*). English laurel is a fast-growing, broad-leafed evergreen tree that is most frequently used as a hedge until it outgrows the persistence of the hedge-pruning crew and becomes a towering thicket. English ivy is more furtive, covering vast expanses of ground at first, then scrambling up and engulfing everything vertical, including fences, trees, and houses. For people who like the bold scale of English laurel leaves but are leery of its growth rate, I would suggest *Photinia* x *Fraseri*, *Ternstroemia gymnanthera*, *Elaeagnus* x *Ebbingei*, or one of the camellia cultivars. For people who just want a broad-leafed evergreen hedge but aren't looking specifically for a large leaf, the options are much greater: several desirable Japanese hollies (*Ilex crenata* vars.), *Osmanthus* species, numerous rhododendrons, *Pyracanthas*, and *Stranvaesias*. For those looking for an ivy substitute,

the list is long and glorious. Just look for groundcovers that don't have tendrils for latching onto nearby vegetation. (If you already have ivy, add ivy control to your maintenance schedule.)

Another way to minimize pruning is to choose plants that will naturally grow in the shape you seek. Do you want a formal appearance, neat and symmetrical? Or do you want a less restrictive, more naturalistic appearance? An Italian cypress (*Cupressus sempervirens*) signals a structured garden, while a vine maple (*Acer circinatum*) evokes a woodland. It would take an inordinate amount of effort to force the vine maple into a formal shape, and an Italian cypress pruned into a rustic shape might look merely odd. If you like the foliage of the Italian cypress but dislike its narrow, upright shape, try one of the irregular-growing junipers, such as *Juniperus chinensis* 'Torulosa' instead, or try the Hinoki false cypress (*Chamaecyparis obtusa* vars). If you want the formal equivalent of a vine maple, consider the hedgerow or Tatar maples (*Acer campestre* and *A. tataricum*), the much-taller sweetgum (*Liquidambar styraciflua*), or even the shrub althaea (*Hibiscus syriacus*), with its late-summer flowers.

Fortunately, most plants can blend into a variety of landscape styles. If a particular plant has some features you like but doesn't blend, you can usually find a substitute that will work better. For the vine maple example above, I assumed that a small, maple-type leaf was of primary importance. But what if an interesting bark is the most important factor, and not the leaf shape? Then perhaps the narrow-growing *Stewartia koreana* or the upright but bushier *S. ovata* would do; their peeling bark isn't green, but it has great wintertime interest.

Nonliving Landscape Elements

We've concentrated so far on maintenance concerns for the living parts of your landscape. But your garden consists of more than plants and trees. We need to focus in on the nonliving elements, such as the wooden structures, mulches, concrete, and watering system, that need tending as well.

WOODEN STRUCTURES: If you live in the Northwest, your garden is likely to include things made of wood: fences, gazebos, decks, footbridges. It's a fact of life that these structures will need maintenance. Still, preventive planning can help. Painted wood requires more maintenance than stained wood. And pressure-treated wood far outlasts untreated wood, especially if the wood will be touching the ground. If you are putting up a wooden fence, you should at the very least use pressure-treated posts. And you will certainly benefit from using pressure-treated wood for decks exposed to the weather. But don't be lulled into thinking that pressure-treated wood needs no further care. Especially when it is to be used in decks, you should consider applying a

---

TIPS ON CHOOSING PLANTS

HOW DO YOU DETERMINE which plants and trees will be suitable candidates for your yard? This kind of detective work can be both instructive and enjoyable.

- Look at what is growing in other people's yards. Note which plants are thriving, and how they are situated. Sun or shade? Near the house or far away?

- Note which plants look like more bother than they are worth. Is that shrub sending out untidy shoots that obviously need pruning? Is that tree buckling the sidewalk? Does that perennial look particularly bug-eaten?

- Check your local library for books and magazines about plants and plantings. Read up especially on topics that relate to your yard. There are many good books on landscaping in shady areas, for instance, but start with George Schenk's *The Complete Shade Gardener* (Houghton Mifflin Company, 1984).

- Get pamphlets from your local agricultural extension agent concerning plants suitable for your area.

- Ask questions at local nurseries.

- Join local plant societies that share your interests.

- Talk to a landscape architect or designer. See Chapter 4, "Landscape Professionals," for more information.

water-repellent sealant, and perhaps a stain as well, to prevent the worst effects of weathering. Most pressure treatments will not by themselves prevent wood from cracking, warping, or splintering. The pressure treatment simply makes the wood resistant to rot and inedible to insects. Structures covered by a roof, such as a gazebo, are less likely to need pressure-treated wood.

If you use pressure-treated wood *and* follow up with periodic applications of stain or sealant, then chances are that you will never have to rebuild the fence, deck, or whatever for as long as you own the house.

You should use a water sealant and/or stain for any untreated wood, whether in fences, decks, gaze-bos, or elsewhere. If you are concerned about the use of chemicals in your yard, you're not completely out of luck. There are environmentally safe stains and sealants on the market, although you may have to look harder for them.

What are the possible drawbacks of using pressure-treated wood? You might want to ask your wood supplier what chemicals have been used to preserve the wood. You won't find much pen-tachlorophenol, or "penta," used these days to treat wood, but you might have some old structures in your yard that have been treated with it, and it's nasty stuff. If you use pressure-treated wood in raised-bed vegetable plantings, then staple polyethy-lene sheeting to the side that will be in contact with

soil so that no chemicals leach into the soil where the roots are. Polyethylene shielding can prolong the life span of untreated wood too.

MULCHES: We use bark mulch, sawdust, and gravel in landscaping partly for appearance and partly for weed control. Don't expect any of them to give you total weed control. A fabric weed barrier between the soil and the mulch will help, but you will still get some weeds poking up.

Bark mulch and sawdust will decay over a period of time, making it necessary to reapply them if you want continued weed control. Of the two, bark mulch is more expensive, but it lasts longer and is the mulch most often used in Northwest yards. Most homeowners prefer the look of bark mulch to that of sawdust. One nice feature of these organic mulches is that they contribute to soil quality as they decay. See the section on mulches in Chapter 8, "Site Preparation," for more information.

Gravel is the longest-lasting mulch; it doesn't decay, but it has its own problems. It's easier to pull weeds from bark and sawdust than from gravel. You may also find it difficult to clean up any debris that falls into gravel—debris you might be able to ignore if it fell onto bark. I hope you don't consider using a gravel mulch underneath a big tree, a pine or fir or the like. The leaf or needle fall, which looks so great out in the forest, will look terrible on top of your gravel mulch, and there is no totally effective means of cleaning it up, although hard work with a rake or power blower can help. If you do decide to use gravel around trees, consider using a dark-colored variety so that trapped needles and leaves will be less conspicuous.

Are there any circumstances where a light-colored gravel would be appropriate? Yes, if it fits in with the overall theme of the house and yard, and if you are willing to put up with its shortcomings. One possible solution: Consider using the lighter colors, where appropriate, in exposed aggregate concrete walkways or driveways. You will have the advantage of getting the color scheme you want combined with the relative ease of cleanup of concrete. A broom or a hose could be all you need to keep it looking neat.

CONCRETE: Concrete tends to add a formal note to the landscape, yet it can be shaped into graceful, non-symmetrical curves as well. If you are thinking of using colored concrete, rather than the usual shade of gray, consider using a concrete color additive. The additive is put right into the concrete as it is being mixed, or added as a wet mix after the concrete has been poured and leveled but before it has set so that the color becomes a permanent part of it. If the concrete gets scuffed or chipped, you will not see the original concrete gray showing through underneath. Or you could use an exposed aggregate gravel in your concrete mix, as suggested above. Either of these methods has a distinct advantage over rolling a layer of paint onto plain concrete. Paint does eventually chip or peel, forcing you to scrape and repaint periodically.

Any concrete can become a victim of moss encroachment, especially in the Northwest. Moss is most active in wet, shady spots, but can take up residence even in the sun. If you don't control it with periodic sweeps with a broom, it can ruin the concrete. No concrete is truly maintenance-free.

IRRIGATION: Sprinkler systems can require upkeep as well. But I don't begrudge the time spent taking care of mine because I know it's time well-invested. If I take care of the irrigation system, my plants won't die for lack of water. Maintenance chores include regular inspecting for clogged or malfunctioning sprinkler heads, broken pipes, and timer settings. Make sure that areas are getting proper amounts of water—not too much, not too little.

◆ ◆ ◆

Depending upon your particular situation, you may have other landscape features in mind that will need maintenance too. You will benefit greatly if you examine each of them with the same critical eye we've used in the rest of this chapter, balancing usefulness of each item against its potential drain on your time and pocketbook.

CHAPTER SIX

Design Principles

Creating a
Unified Landscape

I first saw a hybrid Rolls-Volkswagen about 20 years ago. It was a plain Volkswagen bug onto which was grafted the distinctive front end of an imitation Rolls-Royce. The grillwork and hood section came from a kit and was bolted on in place of the bug's original modest snub nose. This

62

kind of chimera has a certain amount of aesthetic shock value, but the element of surprise wears off and you're left with an irritating juxtaposition of images.

Similarly, it is possible to put any type of landscaping around any type of house. But why do so, unless you want to spite your neighbors? Although the net effect might not be as jolting as a Volks-Royce, a poor matchup of architectural style with landscaping style can detract from a house's value and appearance. That is why, although this is a book on Northwest landscaping, I'm not going to suggest that every yard west of the Cascades be landscaped in some rigidly defined, mythical Northwest style, complete with the botanical equivalent of a flannel shirt and down vest. What's more important is that your landscaping, whatever style you choose, should look as if it belongs.

Fortunately, this aim shouldn't be too hard to accomplish. The easiest way to achieve it is to seek out and use a unifying theme. There are few feelings more satisfying than the sense that things belong together. You can unify your landscaping by:

- Keeping it simple;
- Matching the yard to the architecture of the house;
- Grouping plants by family, geography, or climate;
- Working within an established landscaping style that has proven successful in our area.

I started this chapter by overstating the case. Yes, things can look awkward when we mismatch the landscaping with the house, or mix up landscape plants or elements so that they argue with each other. But there is room for flexibility too. Sometimes a clear, inventive vision can justify a change in the "rules." Sometimes sheer necessity (impending lack of water, for instance) can do the same thing. Whoever would have thought 20 years ago that so many of us would suddenly be interested in drought-tolerant plants from the Mediterranean, California, and Australia? In Chapter 7, "Visions of the Garden," you will see gardens that challenge some of the assumptions we once made about what's appropriate in particular settings or with particular architectural styles. So start with the rules and make yourself familiar with them; then, if you are so inclined, fit them into your own vision. Think of creativity as the combination of familiar elements in new, unexpected ways. If you can make something new, unexpected, and attractive, so much the better.

There are few feelings more satisfying than the sense that things belong together.

Keeping It Simple

This is easy advice to give, although it might be difficult to take. If you are a beginning designer, try to limit your plant choices (as well as your choices of structural materials) to a favorite, appropriate few. At the very practical level, it is easier to blend plantings successfully if you have fewer ingredients in the botanical stew. You'll be better off using groups of identical or similar plants, rather than an isolated specimen of each plant that charms you at the plant sale or the nursery. You then have the added advantage of not having to learn several different, and sometimes contradictory, sets of plant-care instructions. Garden furniture, structures, and ornaments, too, should look as if they belong to the same century and continent. A Japanese water basin, no matter how beautiful, probably doesn't belong next to an Italian bas-relief pot. And a modern abstract bronze may appear awkward near an Egyptian "relic."

♦

At the practical level, it's easier to blend plantings successfully if you have fewer ingredients in the botanical stew.

♦

If you are a plant collector or enthusiast, this suggested limitation will probably seem like a straitjacket. It can be hard to keep any sense of organization in your yard if your green thumb starts itching whenever you pass a nursery, or whenever you read news of an upcoming plant sale by one of your area's many specialty plant societies. This urge can blossom into collectoritis, where you end up with one of this, one of that—and if you run out of room,

you start hoping that something will die so that you'll have room for just one more plant.

But there are ways you can channel this tendency, and even make it work in your favor. You will need to exercise some self-control. You will have to start conservatively and broaden your palette as your knowledge and confidence grow. One thing is clear: If you have a limited budget but exuberant tastes, it is easier to experiment with different combinations of annuals and perennials than with woody plants and trees. The section below on grouping plants by family, geography, or climate explains some ways of organizing the plant life in your garden so that things fit together well.

Matching Your Yard Scheme to Your House

I will freely acknowledge that not every Northwest home has a clear architectural style; many of our older houses were built by people without much formal training or interest in following an established trend, and many newer homes exhibit a mixture of design styles. Still, you might find that your house fits in some sense into one of the broad categories below. If so, you have a useful hint to help you in planning your landscape.

There are three basic living environments to consider: urban, suburban, and rural. City dwellers, unless they live in one of the more exclusive enclaves or close to the city limits, are often elbow-to-elbow with their neighbors. Lot sizes are small, and houses are often sized to match—unless you live in areas where "monster houses" have sneaked past zoning regulations.

Unlike so many Eastern cities, Northwest cities have very few row houses. Instead, most homeowners live in single, detached dwellings. Some of the smallest houses are bungalows and cottages. Their façades are often symmetrical, with matching front windows flanking a small porch and front door. (Urban houses are also apt to be older than houses in the suburbs, although "old" to a Northwesterner almost always refers to a house built between 1900 and 1930.) Between the house and the paved street will be a concrete sidewalk; between the sidewalk and the street curb there is likely to be a parking strip, typically planted in lawn. Frequently there are formal, symmetrical plantings in the yard that echo the symmetry of the house itself. In this small, symmetrical context, care must be taken that the garden does not outshine the house; dwarf conifers, evergreen azaleas, boxwood, and annual bedding-plant flowers work well.

Larger, older urban estates can make superb backdrops for elaborate formal gardens; bricks, interlocking concrete pavers, and refined ironwork blend well with this setting. For more modern urban homes, great or small, an Asian influence in the garden can be most welcome.

In the suburbs, houses are more likely to be ramblers, with rough red-cedar siding and cedar shake or composition roofs. Until a few years ago, most suburban houses were built on lots ranging from 7,000 to 15,000 square feet. This gave homeowners a chance to stretch out a bit, to plant a large lawn and large shrubbery areas, to install a pool or hot tub or sport court, and to park a motor home or boat in the side yard, behind a fence. Landscaping in the suburbs is more likely to be informal or naturalistic, in keeping with the informality of the architecture and surroundings. Sometimes a less-rigid version of Japanese landscaping can be appropriate.

As the cost of land rises and land availability decreases, however, newer houses in the suburbs are being built on smaller and smaller lots. This lot-size squeeze will inevitably have an effect on how we approach suburban landscaping; lawns will shrink, and smaller plants will become more appropriate. So will the trend in some of these developments toward Tudor-style house stylings with faux–leaded-glass windows. Expect to see landscaping with more English or Continental accents to match the architecture in these neighborhoods.

Out in the rural areas, the primary common feature seems to be space—lots of it. You will see plenty of suburban-style houses, sheltered by towering Douglas firs or buffered by pastureland. But you will also see an occasional mobile home, log cabin, farmhouse, or geodesic dome. You will find that the neighbors are as likely to be stockbrokers as dairy farmers. This is an environment where a fruit orchard, a large berry patch, and an ambitious food garden can be established if maintenance time allows, without concern about available space. For the traditional farmhouse, you could consider as well some of the old favorites—deciduous shrubs such as forsythia, mock-orange (*Philadelphus* spp.), and snowball (*Viburnum opulus* 'Sterile')—surrounding a large lawn.

Grouping Plants

PLANT FAMILIES: Is there a particular family of plants to which you are partial—for example, the rose family? Narrowly defined, that would include only the genus *Rosa*—all the familiar hybrid teas, floribundas, grandifloras, and miniature roses, plus the shrub roses and old garden roses. Just concentrating on roses as the foundation of their garden plantings is enough to keep many people happy. Others might widen their scope to cover other members of the family Rosaceae, including the genera *Prunus* (cherries, plums, almonds, peaches, apricots, the aggressive English and Portugal laurel, and so on), *Rubus* (blackberries, raspberries, and some choice groundcovers), *Malus* (apples and crabapples), *Pyrus* (European and Asian pears), *Fragaria* (strawberries), plus cotoneaster, pyracantha, and the ubiquitous photinia—the list continues. Although the family resemblance is not always apparent, one advantage of staying within the group is that a good portion of them have the same cultural requirements: a neutral to slightly alkaline soil and a fertilizer to match.

Another favorite plant family in the Northwest is the heath family, Ericaceae. This family includes the heaths and heathers (the genera *Erica, Calluna, Daboecia, Cassiope, Bruckenthalia,* and *Phyllodoce* are widely used), *Arctostaphylos* (kinnikinnick and manzanita), *Arbutus* (strawberry tree and madrona), *Enkianthus* (bellflower tree), *Gaultheria* (wintergreen and salal), *Pieris, Rhododendron* (including azaleas), and *Vaccinium* (including lingonberry, blueberry, huckleberry, and cranberry). Again, it would be easy

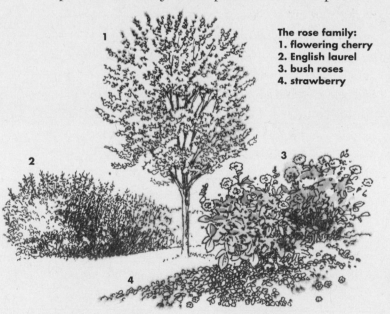

The rose family:
1. flowering cherry
2. English laurel
3. bush roses
4. strawberry

to plant an entire yard using mostly these and other close relatives from this one family, although this time you would want to make sure the soil is on the acid side and use fertilizers formulated for acid-loving plants. Most of these plants, except the *Arctostaphylos*, prefer a generous supply of water. There is such variety in the heath family that no gardener should have to complain of boredom.

Some collectors devote their gardens to primarily one genus of plants. This is why we have so many specialty plant societies in our area for fanciers of rhododendrons, chrysanthemums, primulas, dahlias, and lilies, to name just a few. Still other gardeners like to include broad groupings of plants in their gardens: perennials, ferns, ornamental grasses, hardy bulbs, or alpines.

GEOGRAPHICAL AND CLIMATE GROUPINGS: You might also want to unify the planting theme of your garden in other ways. Depending upon the overall landscaping style you prefer, geographic specificity can help tie things together. One good teaching example of such a plan is the geographical garden near the stadium at the University of British Columbia, in Vancouver, B.C. It is divided into sections displaying hardy or near-hardy plants from several continents: Europe, Asia, North America, South America, and so on. In Seattle, the University of Washington is creating a similar "plant map" over much of its campus.

The heath family:
1. madrona
2. rhododendron
3. azalea (rhododendron)
4. kinnikinnick

An obvious—and highly practical—geographical choice would be to use a generous percentage of native Northwest plants in your landscape. Native plants are likely to grow well in your yard, and many of them will be readily available at decent prices. (A few plants, such as our beautiful madrona, *Arbutus Menziesii*, are difficult to transplant, so nurseries are reluctant to carry them.) If you prefer some Japanese influence in your landscaping, then it makes perfect sense to use a good number of plants—and ornaments—of Japanese origin. Plants from a particular region can be used as a subtle means of evoking a specific response in viewers of your garden.

A related approach to unifying your landscape plan is to group plants from similar environments.

PLANT COMMUNITIES

ONE INTERESTING METHOD of blending plants together in a landscape is to imitate plant groupings found in wilderness areas nearby. Here are three sample plant lists taken from widely divergent spots in the Northwest. In each case, the plants mentioned grow within a 50-foot radius of each other. Note that the listing for Foster Island, a wildlife reserve within the city limits of Seattle, has a high percentage of non-native plants that have escaped from cultivation.

**A small salt-water island
in the San Juans:**
Arbutus Menziesii (madrona)
Lonicera sp. (honeysuckle)
Mahonia aquifolium
    (Oregon grape)
Polypodium scouleri
    (one of the licorice ferns)
Pseudotsuga Menziesii
    (Douglas fir)
Sedum spathulifolium (stonecrop)
Symphoricarpos albus (snowberry)

**Foster Island in
Lake Washington:**
Iris pseudacorus (yellow flag—
    an introduced plant)
Juncus sp. (bog rush)
Lythrum sp. (loosestrife—
    an introduced weed)

Nymphaea sp. (water lily—
    an introduced plant)
Salix sp. (willow)
Spirea Douglasii (hardhack spirea)
Typha latifolia (cattail)

Woods near Lake Wenatchee:
Acer circinatum (vine maple)
Acer glabrum (Rocky Mountain
    maple, Douglas maple)
Ceanothus velutinus (wild lilac)
Linnaea borealis (twinflower)
Mahonia repens
    (creeping mahonia)
Pachystima myrsinites (false box)
Pinus contorta latifolia
    (lodgepole pine)
Pseudotsuga Menziesii
    (Douglas fir)
Sambucus glauca (blue elderberry)

Even if the plants originated in widely separate places on the globe, they will often look right together. If the environment in your garden allows, you might specialize in plants from woodland, meadow, swamp or streamside, alpine barrens, or dry prairie regions. I recently visited a garden that contained mostly native Northwest woodland plants—but mixed in with the natives were some styrax trees and hostas originally from wooded regions of Japan, groupings of hybrid rhododendrons from several continents, and alpine strawberries, or *fraises des bois* (*Fragaria* sp.), from the forests of France. Another garden I visited recently was an urban cottage garden, where many of the plants were drought-resistant Mediterranean and Australian natives. I saw a great deal of gray, blue, and silver foliage typical of dryland plants from around the world—and they all looked comfortable in each other's company. The advantage to both of these approaches is obvious: The woodland plants require woodland care, and the dryland plants require sun and little water. (See Chapter 7, "Visions of the Garden," the Story and Kyper gardens.) At work here is the principle of grouping plants with similar care needs together.

A Unifying Style

One convenient way to make the elements of your garden work together successfully is to emulate an existing landscape style. This isn't absolutely necessary; many superb gardens are best described as eclectic. But perhaps you could begin with a particular style and improvise on the theme, making something recognizable but definitely your own. Here are some of the formal and informal design styles popular in the Northwest.

THE CONTINENTAL OR EUROPEAN GARDEN: Many larger Northwest houses are modeled after styles originating in Europe or England. If they have brick facades, careful window detailing, or other architectural references to European tradition, then certainly formal European landscaping would be appropriate. But even a modest house, provided its architecture is more or less symmetrical, can benefit from this approach. Here are the typical features of this landscaping style in its purest form:

* Expect geometric repetition of lines and forms. Look for circles, squares, rectangles, triangles, and patterns as regular as the meters of classical poetry. "Tree-shrub-shrub-tree-shrub-shrub" might be one example. Pools and waterways will follow the rules of regularity too.

* Both the hardscape features and the living plants are kept in well-disciplined order. In extreme cases, the natural contours of the land will be reshaped to meet the demands of the design. Plants either should have strong architectural features by nature or should be eminently trimmable. (Note that extensive pruning translates into high maintenance.)

* Ornamentation, such as statuary and plant containers, tends toward the classical European or the mythological.

* Large masses are used for effect. This style might not seem like a promising one for a collector's garden, but it can work. You can build a formal framework of hedges and edgings, and place favorite plants, organized by theme (perennials, for example) or family if possible, into the formal "containers."

* Topiary pruning is used for certain specimens. Leafy or mossy deer with antlers, men on horseback, and doves appear to wander through the formal confines of the garden.

THE JAPANESE GARDEN: It is presumptuous to try to summarize Japanese landscaping in just a few paragraphs. What follows is not a definitive description of Japanese landscape style. Instead, I will list some of its better-known elements, which can be useful in many Northwest gardens even where the architecture of the associated house is not specifically Japanese. If you become deeply interested in the subject, I hope you will look into Katsuo Saito and Sadaji Wada's *Magic of Trees and Stone: Secrets of Japanese Gardening* (JPT Book Company, 1964). At the risk of oversimplification, then, here are some guiding principles as they might apply to our region:

* Shapes and textures are typically more important

than flowers. Those blooms that do appear are likely to be soft, quiet, cool colors rather than strident tones—Helen Hayes rather than Bette Midler.

- Structural elements are more likely to be asymmetrical. Expect to see winding pathways, not straight avenues.
- The effect is naturalistic—which is not the same as natural. Gardens are a representation of certain features found in nature, and the representation may be highly stylized.
- There is frequent use of rocks and water. Rocks are often organized in traditional patterns, using a familiar "vocabulary," so that they tell stories to those who can read the stones. Broken or sharp-featured rocks represent discord or dynamism; smooth, weathered rocks bring peace and repose to the garden. Water may be actually present, contained in pools or stone basins, or it may be implied by dry streambeds lined with washed rock. If there is room for real water, then there's room for koi or other fish.
- Trees and shrubs may be pruned loosely and informally, or tightly sheared—but in either case the pruning will be asymmetrical. (Straight, formal border hedges, which could look as if they were transplanted from an Italian villa, are an exception.

Left: Everything is balanced in this European garden. Each corner of the rectangular space has a pot of heliotrope. The brick patio has symmetrical cutouts for plants, which are repeated regularly. Narrow, upright pyramidalis add another formal touch. (Design by Withey-Price Landscape Design)

Some of the heavier shearing can have an almost topiary flavor—the Asian counterpart of the more symmetrical formal European garden.)

- A yard is typically divided into several smaller gardens, each with its own purpose. On the street side, visitors enter through a gate into a small enclosed courtyard. The main garden areas are at the rear of the house.
- Ornamentation is important: bridges, stone lanterns, stone basins with dipping cups. The high cost of carved stone means that most Japanese-style ornamentation in our country is made from cast concrete instead.
- Size is unimportant—even the tiniest space can become a Japanese landscape.

In Japan itself, some landscaping shows signs of influence from other cultures, both stylistically and in terms of the plants used. Tulips and salvias in a Japanese garden? Straight pathways and walls? It can happen. And these gardens can give us clues about how to adapt Japanese landscaping to Northwest needs.

THE NORTHWEST STYLE: I've claimed in the introduction to this book that Northwest landscaping encompasses an attitude rather than a single specific approach. Still, let's try to describe a typical Northwest garden:

- It is rooted in respect and admiration for the natural

THE DESIGN SPECTRUM

WE CAN BROADLY SAY that landscaping can be either formal, naturalistic, or chaotic. A formal garden is more likely to have a high degree of symmetry in its elements, and perhaps a high level of structure too. Plants are used almost as substitute "structures." In a naturalistic landscape, the trees and plants should look as if they really or plausibly could grow together in the wild. A naturalistic garden has fewer structures, and less obvious symmetry, but there can be as much attention paid to the balancing of different elements there as in the formal garden—or even more. The spectrum from formal to naturalistic is a wide one, with lots of options along the way.

A chaotic garden, on the other hand, ignores all pretense of organization. It is merely an accretion of details. This kind of garden is made up of one of this and one of that. It is also an unnecessary garden, since even a staunch collector can do some planning, both before and during the process of collecting, to keep the different details balanced. As landscape architect Bud Merrill points out, a natural garden is not a chaotic one. Nature is not chaotic. Specific plants congregate in those areas most suited to them.

features and plants native to this area.

♦ It leans toward a naturalistic rather than a formal context, but spans a range of structuralism from simple to complex. If the associated house is asymmetrical, then structures such as decks and patios tend to be asymmetrical too.

♦ It often contains echoes of the Japanese landscape style, with informal, winding pathways and plant groupings.

♦ There is a fondness for color, but the shape of each plant is important as well. Flowering bulbs are popular and especially effective in irregular sweeps or drifts.

♦ Less emphasis on pruning than in either the European or the Japanese garden means less maintenance.

♦ Traditionally, there has been a fondness for lawn; this is the one high-maintenance item.

♦ Native trees and shrubs, and other plants that look as if they might be native, are often used to create a wilder touch within an otherwise civilized garden. A plethora of rhododendrons has entered on the coattails of our native *Rhododendron macrophyllum*, as well as Douglas fir, Western hemlock, and numerous junipers.

Right: There is not one straight line in this entire Japanese-style garden. Instead, we see irregular masses of foliage interspersed with spikes of daylily. Tall trees from a back-yard greenbelt enhance the informal—but not strictly naturalistic—tone. (Design by Jerry Munro)

COUNTRY OR PERENNIAL GARDEN: An ongoing fascination with things British brings us to the most colorful gardens we see in the Northwest:

◆ Color is the dominant element. Roses, annuals, and perennials, in their seasons, bring immense amounts of color, and often fragrance.

◆ Plants are frequently chosen more for their leaf or flower color than for their shape or their off-season appearance. An English country garden needs special forethought or it will look barren when the weather turns cold.

◆ Much of the planting is evanescent, requiring either periodic replanting as the previous season's plantings begin to decline, or complex interplanting to achieve a long period of continuous color.

◆ Increased maintenance is required if the plants have difficult or contradictory care requirements. Most gardens in this style will require more work than a naturalistic Northwest or Japanese landscape.

◆ You can start a perennial garden for much less money than most other gardens, because you can work with inexpensive seeds or small starter plants. But the costs will skyrocket if you get hooked on rare perennials.

◆ Size is not important. The garden can be either large or tiny.

◆ The country garden can be adapted to an environment that is highly structured (formal), less structured (informal), or even naturalistic.

Obviously, more landscape styles exist than those noted above, and you certainly don't need to limit yourself to one of these few. But perhaps you've seen something of your own tastes reflected in the descriptions. In the next chapter you'll see some examples of gardens that use these styles as starting points and then go on to make strong landscaping statements.

CHAPTER SEVEN

Visions of the Garden

Representative
Northwest
Landscapes

When we make a conscious effort to build a garden—when we resist the temptation to just go along and instead decide to put our own personal stamp on our surroundings—then we begin to design a garden that reflects not only our own personality but perhaps even our vision of what Paradise looks like. Though we may build gardens with some practical purposes in mind, a real garden expresses something about what delights or moves us.

It shouldn't be any surprise, then, that none of the gardens I describe below fits neatly into a single pattern. Each reflects the individual vision of the homeowners, developed by themselves or with the help of professionals working to give voice to their aspirations. Some of the gardens are peaceful, and others are exuberant. I have tried to label each garden as I describe it, but since these are real-life gardens, they don't always fit neatly into categories.

The Leahy Garden:
Northwest Naturalistic

Sometimes natural forces leap out and take control of a landscape project. When you build a home over a stream, the stream will dominate the proceedings. Jack and Maggie Leahy discovered this in their rural hideaway in urban Seattle, one block away from a street that carries over 10,000 cars a day. Their Baba Yaga–style house, split into two sections joined by a suspended passageway-entrance, lies lengthwise down the course of the stream. The year-round watercourse runs from the upper west portion of the yard, goes under one section of the house, flows beneath the passageway, plunges under the lower section of the house, and emerges into the lower front yard, where it leaves the property under the roadway to the east.

The Leahys had planted a lawn on the banks of the stream, but it had never thrived. A dense, damp soil and abundant shade conspired against it, and the English ivy (*Hedera helix*) and wild morning glory at the edges kept creeping in to cover both the lawn and all the other vegetation. The house, filled with books and guests and talk of distant places, was being engulfed.

Six years ago, the Leahys decided to regain control of their yard. They asked me for some advice. We began by taking a tentative inventory of existing plants, to see what could be salvaged from the ivy. What emerged first was a large, tangled crabapple tree, close to the roadway. Several evergreen azaleas and rhododendrons also hid within the ivy, and a number of sword ferns (*Polystichum munitum*) and lady ferns (*Athyrium filix-femina*) were doing just fine. A boulevard cypress (*Chamaecyparis pisifera* 'Cyanoviridis') had struggled for several years and given up, as had a wooden bridge across the stream. The ivy had scrambled up many of the numerous native trees in the yard, including some large Western red cedars (*Thuja plicata*) and several substantial bigleaf maples (*Acer macrophyllum*). The ivy had killed one cluster of the maples and was bent on killing the rest. But then, ivy's main purpose is to smother other plants and hide the evidence.

The water created some situations that needed attention. On the east side, the stream was eroding

VISIONS OF THE GARDEN 77

the bank of soil that supported the street beyond. The drainage culvert that was supposed to capture the water was instead being undermined by the erosion. And the house itself, although it never flooded because it sat so high above the stream, was sometimes nearly surrounded by water when the flow exceeded the capacity of the culvert that went under the house. At moments like these, from some angles, the house looked like a ship headed upstream.

The three biggest problems of the yard, then, were ivy, water, and shade. What were the best features? Water, the crabapple, many shade-making trees, and the astonishing illusion that the house was in a forest and not in the city. We decided that the yard should capitalize upon this, and agreed to steer away from too many "cultivated" touches. We also decided to divide the project into two parts, corresponding to the front and back of the house, and to concentrate on the front yard first.

I suggested that the invasive ivy should go: away from the tree trunks, out of the shrubbery, and off the ground. It stayed in only one spot in the yard, on the northern slope, where it could do battle with the blackberry briars reaching from an under-maintained rental house next door. After the ivy was gone, we discovered that a few of the rhododendrons and several bright pink azaleas were salvageable, and we decided to use them elsewhere in the yard.

We chose to approach the water situation from several angles. The first phase of the landscape proj-

ect focused only on the lower length of the stream, from the point where the water emerges from beneath the house to where it goes under the street below. From a campground creek near Lake Quinault Lodge, I adapted the idea of a gabion, a wire cage filled with cobbles, to contain the erosion near the culvert. In the soil behind the gabion, I planted peppermint and spearmint, hoping that their aggressive roots would help to slow erosion by holding the soil together.

The invasive ivy had to go: away from tree trunks, out of shrubbery, off the ground.

After checking with surface-water management authorities to make sure that this was not a fish-bearing stream, I modified the course of the water by carving out some of the bends in the streambed to make them more pronounced and placing groups of deflecting and damming rocks along the length of the stream. This was done in part for visual effect but also to increase the water-sounds the stream made.

Where the wooden bridge had been, I used some additional flat-topped rock as a stepping-stone bridge. Perpendicular to the stream, and meeting it at the stepping stones, was a pathway of flat stepping stones that would eventually wind around one entire side of the house. The bottom and sides of the stream I lined with cobbles and washed gravel. (While my co-worker, Chris Merrill, and I were disturbing the stream, we put up screens of DuPont Mirafi™ filter to minimize the water turbidity downstream.) I added a few Siberian iris and lemon daylilies (*Hemerocallis lil-ioasphodelus*) along the edge, but most of the bank was already lined with lady fern, which remained and flourished.

We used
the evergreen
magnolia, less fussy
than our native
madrona, but with
similar dark,
shiny leaves.

I recommended the removal of most of the bigleaf maples. I argued that they were making the house too shaded, creating moss problems on the roof and darkness inside the house. I was outvoted on this, but a few of the maples that had become unsafe did get taken down.

Near the front-yard stream, I added two small trees—an upright form of mugho pine (*Pinus mugo*) and a katsura tree (*Cercidiphyllum japonicum*)—to minimize noise and visibility of traffic and to increase privacy. A pyramidalis (*Thuja occidentalis* 'Pyramidalis') hedge across the front completed the sense of enclosure. A few compact rhododendrons (*R. Wardii* and *R.* 'Crest'), three *Pieris japonica*, three lambkill (*Kalmia angustifolia*), some coralberry (*Symphoricarpos orbicula-tus*) and native Oregon oxalis (*O. oregana*) for additional erosion control, and a lone Hinoki cypress (*Chamaecyparis obtusa* 'Gracilis') filled out the plant list. After all the planting was done, we spread two to three inches of bark mulch to keep down the weeds until the groundcovers filled in.

It may sound bizarre to think of installing a sprinkler system so near to a stream, but the plants would clearly need watering, at least for the first few years. To simplify this chore, I put in a one-zone system consisting of two impulse sprinklers on 3-foot-high risers. They were connected via white PVC pipe to a short length of regular garden hose attached to a hose bibb.

Six years later, most of the front-yard design works. Some extremely dry summers convinced the Leahys that they needed to get extra water to the pyramidalis, so they laid out a soaker hose to direct water right to the roots of the hedge. All of the perennials, including the ferns, oxalis, daylilies, and Siberian iris, have thrived. Some unexpected changes have occurred to the stream, most of them caused by an upstream property owner who allowed massive amounts of freshly graded dirt to wash into the stream, causing much of the Leahys' course to silt up. And although the ivy has not returned in any quantity to the lower yard, morning glory still pops up and demands attention. Overall, this qualifies as a low-maintenance front yard, requiring some fall cleanup of maple leaves and occasional weeding during the warmer months.

The back yard presented a more difficult design challenge. Four neighboring houses looked down upon it, and a new mini-shopping mall was just being constructed. What could have been a private area was instead rather exposed. It had a healthy bamboo hedge, but most of the rest of it was wild grass. After cleaning out the weeds, we decided to build multiple pools, constructed of benite, quick-setting concrete, and rock, for the uphill side of the stream.

My brother, Bill Munro of Rose Hill Landscaping, designed and installed the changes to this section of the stream, and added some grace notes as well. For one side of the house, he designed and installed a 12-inch-diameter overflow tube to help minimize the uncontrolled washouts when the stream rises beyond its banks.

After the stream changes were made, I installed numerous ferns and hostas along the stream's banks. Farther away, I planted a few rhododendrons, a fragrant-flowered evergreen magnolia (*M. grandiflora* 'Victoria'), and a hedge of chartreuse-gold Castlewellan cypress (x *Cupressocyparis Leylandii* 'Castlewellan') to screen off the new construction up the hill, since it didn't look as if the bamboo would be sufficient to do the job. We used the magnolia because it has a dark, shiny leaf similar to that of our native madrona (*Arbutus Menziesii*), but is much less fussy as a garden plant. I intended to remove the bamboo when the Castlewellan cypress grew tall enough in just a few years. We also put in a very high welded-wire fence to support a scrambling honey-suckle vine (*Lonicera sempervirens*).

The vine has now matured to the point where it covers the fence and hides much of the new construc-tion. Surprisingly (to me), the Castlewellan cypress didn't work very well. The plants grew quickly, but without much stem or root strength, and now they flop about, perhaps because the back yard is shaded for half the day. The bamboo has worked very well indeed, and now, with the honeysuckle, provides excellent screening. So, the bamboo stays and the cypress must go. And the evergreen magnolia? As sometimes happens in the Northwest, a burden of snow did some natural pruning. We persist in plant-ing evergreen magnolias here because they give us such pleasure. The back-yard portion of the stream silted up as much as the front yard, but still looks and sounds fine. With the abundant ferns and hostas, it remains the focal point from within the west side of the house, framed by a large picture window visible from much of the house through a long hallway.

The Flakus Garden: Northwest Eclectic

Across Lake Washington in Kirkland is another example of naturalistic Northwest landscaping, this time designed by my father, Jerry Munro. The Flakus front yard qualifies as a low-maintenance landscape: There is no lawn, and, nearly a decade after it was originally planted, the yard has needed no major pruning or thinning. The land is shaped into two rolling berms, divided by an irregular pathway.

Continued on page 91

Northwest Landscapes

Perennial Gardens

1. A crushed gravel path curves through botanical splendor. In the foreground, a jaunty pink evening primrose (*Oenothera Berlandieri* 'Siskiyou') spills into the pathway. A tall plume poppy (*Macleaya microcarpa*) looms in the background on the right. The rest of this garden features undulating waves of foliage and flower, punctuated by blades of *Yucca flaccida* 'Ivory Towers' and *Iris siberica* 'Tropic Night.' (Design by Withey-Price Landscape Design)

2. A simple clay pot filled with seasonal color. Geraniums and nasturtiums share space with blades of fiery crocosmia. (Design by Lisa Hummel)

3. A midsummer feast of color and scent hides the formal backbone of this garden. Note the upright golden yews, regular globes of dwarf boxwood, the symmetrical trellis frame, and the straight grass pathway that ends in a T at the center of the house. (Design by Withey-Price Landscape Design)

4. Brick edging keeps grass pathway from intruding into the narrow planting areas on either side of the path. A slow-growing, golden-leaved full-moon maple (*Acer japonicum* 'Aureum') and a rose-pink columbine (*Aquilegia* sp.) brighten the side of the house, and a fragrant honeysuckle vine (*Lonicera* sp.) covers the chimney. (Design by Susan Buckles)

5. A sunny Provence garden, transplanted to the Northwest. Several varieties of oregano color the foreground; vertical junipers and olive-leafed willow (*Salix eleagnos*) stand in for the less-suitable Italian cypress and true olive. (Design by Rick Kyper)

6. In the foregound, gray-leafed *Helichrysum Fontanesii* mingles with lavender-and-white-flowered *Scutelleria incana*. Dutch iris 'Bronze Elegance' and some David Austin roses punctuate the middle distance. Beyond them is the rich purple of *Salvia nemerosa*. At the far side of the gravel, we see the foliage blades of *Agapanthus* 'Bressingham Blue' and the daylily 'Sunday Gloves' (*Hemerocallis* sp.). The gray color near the golden mint is from *Stachys lanata* 'Cotton Boll.' The silvery groundcover is an eager *Acaena* species. (Design by Rick Kyper)

7. This planting corner sits level with the lawn, which then slopes away from it toward the street. The planting scheme demonstrates a very clear layering effect—from the golden creeping jenny, grassy *Carex comans* 'Silver Edge,' and red and white dianthus along the rockery, to the creamy yarrows (*Achillea taygetea* and darker *Achillea* 'Moonshine') in the middle, to the tall spikes of delphinium and foxglove in the back. In winter, most of the foliage dies down to reveal a split-rail cedar fence. (Design by Susan Buckles)

Formal Gardens

8. A pyramidalis hedge serves as a backdrop to this small

Captions continued on page 89

Perennial
Gardens

1

2

3

4

5

6

7

8

9

10

Naturalistic
Gardens

11

12

13

14

15

Garden
Structures

16

17

18

19

20

21

22

23

Japanese
Gardens

24

25

26

27

Captions continued from page 80

European garden court that overlooks an extensive formal garden below (shown in photos 1 and 3). Grayish germander *(Teucrium)* is repeated in regular patterns. The decorative pots are filled with complementary-colored plants, appropriate to the seasons: Spring tulips have given way to purple heliotrope. Golden creeping jenny brightens the foreground. (Design by Withey-Price Landscape Design)

9. Raised railroad-tie beds and an aboveground irrigation system simplify maintenence of these generally demanding hybrid roses. A rare dove tree *(Davidia involucrata)* graces the left corner; a Royal Purple smoke tree *(Cotinus coggygria* var.) and compact 'Rosa Mundi' rhododendrons extend the garden's color season. (Design by Bill Munro, Rose Hill Landscaping)

10. Creamy sandstone squares, a perfectly round pool, and a pyramidalis hedge give a structured background to this perennial-rich garden. (Design by Withey-Price Landscape Design)

Naturalistic Gardens

11. A private reading chair nestles in a corner of a brick patio. (Design by landscape architect Keith Geller)

12. An alpine scene in an urban setting: A weathered high-altitude hemlock shades a multilevel granite pool with waterfalls. Tough, flexible PVC lines the pool bottom. (Design by Douglas Reymore of Cascade Construction and Bill Munro of Rose Hill Landscaping)

13. A mature rhododendron and a large shrub rose frame a small pool hiding near a back-yard fence. (Design by Susan Buckles)

14. This natural-color gazebo looks perfectly at home, sur-rounded by towering Western red cedars, Douglas firs, and the understory growth of sword ferns, salal, and red huckleberry. (Landscape design by Bud Merrill, landscape architect)

15. More native plants form the background for this small clearing in a front yard. A wicker chair, and wicker baskets and an antique wagon filled with geraniums, pansies, and lobelia, add a rustic note. (Landscape design by Bud Merrill)

Garden Structures

16. Bronzy, grasslike *Carex flagellifera* interrupt a broken-chunk concrete walkway. Creeping thyme is one of the groundcovers used to fill in between concrete pieces. Yellow *Corydalis* and red *Phygelius capensis* add color. (Design by Gil Schieber)

17. Cobbles and rock outcroppings frame a natural stream; Siberian iris provide seasonal color. (Design by Michael Munro)

18. Timber wall and steps of pressure-treated wood give access up a very steep slope and demonstrate the versatility of wood walls. The patio is of interlocking pavers. (Design by Bill Munro)

19. A sturdy arbor frames a patio terrace; the steps are treated wood softened by *Sagina subulata*. Red color comes from the red lacefleaf maple in the foreground, the Royal Purple smoke tree, red carnations near the steps, and red-tipped photinia beyond the wall of iris. (Design by Scott Lankford, landscape architect, Lankford Associates)

20. Looking down from the arbor in the previous photo (19) shows how a kiwi vine *(Actinidia chinensis)* on a large, free-standing support can minimize the massiveness of the chimney. The red of the brick is picked up by the smoke

trees and creeping thyme, as well as the bark of the madronas in the distance. Note the open texture of the fence, designed to let in as much light as possible in the shade below the deck. (Design by Scott Lankford)

21. Iris and autumn-colored vine maple fit into this small hiding-corner overlooking a lake. Note the bench and arbor-like top built into the open-slat fence. (Design by Scott Lankford)

22. Brick planters, a brick patio, and matching fasciae on the façade upgrade the appearance of this house while remaining faithful to the neighborhood and the era when it was built. A strong trellis-fence supports a vigorous wisteria; a red laceleaf Japanese maple and a bigger relative, the green-leafed Japanese maple, add a touch of asymmetrical balance.

23. A rustic arbor with a wicker beehive-basket supports an akebia vine. (Design by Bud Merrill)

Japanese Gardens

24. Sword ferns, daylilies, and a red laceleaf Japanese maple surround a weathered, mossy granite rock and a Japanese pot and lantern. (Design by Jerry Munro)

25. Cedar bender board separates the planting berm from the surrounding black sand; rocks are placed on both sides of the divider. The azaleas have been trimmed in the close style typical of some Japanese landscapes. (Design by Jerry Munro)

26. A narrow-slat fence with contrasting dark posts and top railing give character to this small courtyard next to a driveway. A green-leafed Japanese maple and a white-flowered anemone fit well with the Japanese theme. (Design by Keith Geller)

27. The lower portion of the same yard shown in photo 26 has a different face altogether. A mature red laceleaf Japanese maple dominates the small, narrow area; the low-growing *Sagina* and other groundcovers are designed so as not to compete for space with the maple. The meandering walkway is of thick granite slabs set in sand. The cobbles in the foregound fold down to a dry sump for seasonal runoff. (Design by Keith Geller)

The effect is that of a valley between two foothills. Rather than gravel or concrete, the pathway is made of interlocking, tan octagon-and-square pavers. This demonstrates how flexible these pavers can be: Their edges have been left untrimmed, so that the pathway moves in a curve that matches the offset of the berms, giving an informal air to a design element that might be very formal in other circumstances.

Set into the asymmetrical berms are three very large granite rocks—one to the left of the path, one to the right, and one farther back on the right. My father did not want the rocks to get swallowed up by vegetation as time passed, so he used three- and four-man-sized rocks. Ten years after the installation, they are still quite visible, although the groundcover, brilliant-blue-flowered *Lithodora diffusa*, covers parts of the two front rocks and heather covers much of the third. The groundcover also partially covers and further softens the edges of the pavers.

Most of the remaining plants are either Northwest natives or stand-ins for local favorites. On the right-side berm, closer to the neighbor's fence, is an informal row of native evergreens that provides some screening between the properties. Closer to the pathway is a grouping of salal (*Gaultheria shallon*), *Pieris japonica*, a red laceleaf Japanese maple (*Acer palmatum* 'Ornatum'), and a threadbranch cypress (*Chamaecyparis pisifera* 'Filifera'). To the left is a *Magnolia grandiflora*—which, like the Leahys' tree, also lost its top half in a recent winter. However, it

regrew rapidly enough to cover the damage and now sends out bloom after scented bloom all summer long. Near it is a kousa dogwood (*Cornus kousa*), which looks much like a scaled-down version of our beautiful native Pacific dogwood (*Cornus Nuttallii*), but is very resistant to the dogwood anthracnose disease that has devastated so many of the native dogwoods. The kousa dogwood is also a better size for small gardens. The outer edge of this left-hand berm, near the short driveway, uses more heather and a massed planting of dwarf Michaelmas daisies in front of another grouping of salal and native red huckleberry (*Vaccinium parvifolium*).

The Story Garden: A Woodland Walk

Of the naturalistic gardens in this chapter, this is the most natural. The Storys have a French Provincial–style house set in two acres of mature second-growth woods. Landscape architect Bud Merrill had the task of preserving as much of the wilderness as possible, while allowing for more civilized landscaping around the periphery of the house. He stresses what he calls "the wonderful order of things" as the basis for the woodscape. That's his way of saying that nature is not chaotic, that there are patterns which reveal themselves with study. The Story yard reveals a lot.

A curving crushed-gravel driveway approaches

the muted-gray stucco house through a cluster of second-growth evergreens. A broad swath of alpine strawberries, giving fruit for both people and wild-life, lines the driveway. Even when you stand before the front porch, you cannot see all of the house. It blends in with the surrounding native and domesti-cated trees—including Douglas firs, a group of *Styrax japonicus,* and a large red-leafed Japanese maple (*Acer palmatum* 'atropur-pureum')—and a varied group of rhododendrons. Flowerpots filled with seasonal color pull the eye to the front entrance of the house. To the right of the short front walk-way (one of only two patches of concrete on the property), a wicker chair and an old iron-wheeled wooden cart begin the theme of rustic orna-mentation that continues throughout the yard, tying the different areas together.

Merrill stresses "the wonderful order of things," that nature is not chaotic, but reveals its patterns with study.

Several pathways lead into the woods. The path circling the house to the left is of crushed gravel edged with two-by-fours; most of the others are pure forest duff. Each path winds by circuitous route to a large, natural-color wooden gazebo. Once you are in the gazebo, an antique lantern, a wicker table, and a primitive broom help to confound your sense of time; looking out over the surrounding woods, you find no point of reference to the twentieth century. Although the woods are on a corner lot, the nearby roadways are invisible and inaudible.

At the juncture of two pathways is a glade full of filtered light; it is decorated with a picnic table, an ancient wooden wheelbarrow with a metal wheel, and a few benches. Plants there include native red huckleberry (*Vaccinium parvifolium*), elderberry (*Sambucus racemosa*), sword ferns, mosses, and some discreetly placed polyanthus primroses. Other path-ways reveal a rhododendron grove, a carved wooden elf peering out from a patch of salal and sword fern, old kerosene lanterns, and a gathering area with wicker chairs created by artisans from around the Northwest. It takes some careful thought to deter-mine what is missing from the woods. There are no nettles, blackberries, or horsetail. This is wilderness that has been groomed with care and subtlety.

Near the house, the landscaping is less rustic, but still has numerous ties to the past. At one end of the house, a small lawn area surrounds a formal fountain and pool, edged with shade-loving white impatiens. The other end has a far sunnier aspect, and the land-scaping takes advantage of the light: A second small lawn area half-circles a colorful country garden. A climbing rose soars up to grasp at the iron railing of a second-story balcony. Another wooden wheelbarrow watches from a corner. And a promontory of the far-thest bed presents a display area for a grouping of seasonal flowers in pots.

Barbara Story estimates that she spends about

three to four hours a week maintaining the entire area, augmented by a part-time gardener who comes in twice a week. This does not seem like a great investment in time, considering the size of the property and the returns it gives. People accustomed to the wide-open spaces east of the Cascades or in the Midwest might yearn for more color and light. But for those attuned to the cool repose of the woods, the place provides a sense of enchantment for both children and adults, and a feeling that something vital is being preserved.

The Hepburn Garden: Permanent Landscaping, Japanese Style

In the previous chapter, "Design Principles," I mentioned that Japanese gardens sometimes use rounded rocks and cooler colors to reflect a sense of peace and repose. There is certainly great peacefulness in this Japanese garden, designed in the mid-1960s by my father, Jerry Munro. The Hepburns' house is a one-story rambler, with black clapboard siding alternating with weathered brick of a soft red. The cedar shake roof is natural color. This subdued color scheme continues into the front yard, which uses a large expanse of black sand instead of lawn.

There *is* some bright color in this yard—a large saucer magnolia (*Magnolia* x *Soulangiana*) bears its white-and-purple blooms in early spring, followed by early and midseason evergreen azaleas (*Rhododendron*

hybrids) in two shades of pink, and orange midsummer daylilies *(Hemerocallis)* — but the main color scheme for the plantings is variations on a theme of green. There are a few dark-green groupings of a very dwarf variety of mugho pine (*Pinus mugo*), still under 3 feet high twenty-five years after planting. Opposite the driveway is the soft golden-green of a 15-foot-tall gold threadbranch cypress (*Chamaecyparis pisifera* 'Filifera Aurea'). Several large Tom Thumb arborvitae (*Thuja occidentalis* 'Globosa') form an irregular line to separate the garden from the street. These naturally rounded arborvitae are so slow growing (4 feet tall in a quarter century) that they will stay in scale with the yard for an extraordinarily long time. When not in bloom, the azaleas and daylilies add touches of light green.

Bender boards, doubled for added sturdiness, make a sharp delineation between the level sand areas and the gentle berms of the island planting areas. Weathered granite rocks, with rounded edges and a partial covering of moss and lichen, are used on the berms in several outcropping-style groups of two or three. In two places, the granite rocks breach the separation of sand and berm, interrupting the flow of bender board by jutting out into the sand. This joining of "land" and "sea" is a common refrain in Japanese design. The Hepburns have complemented this theme by adding a few spare Asian ornaments, including a small stone pot, and a Chinese-style owl and Japanese-style crow, both in black iron.

Maintenance is minimal. Not many weeds come up through the black sand, which is separated from the soil underneath by a black plastic barrier. The Hepburns have a gardener come in three times a year to do the little weeding necessary, to pinch back the mugho pines and azaleas, to clean up the daylilies as they decline in the fall, and on rare occasion, to thin out the saucer magnolia.

Seeing this garden again after many years reminds me that every landscape has its own life cycle. It grows, matures, and flourishes for a period of time, and then eventually outgrows its bounds. Its useful lifespan is determined partly by how well it is maintained, but primarily by the choice and placement of plants. If, like the Hepburns, you are interested in creating a permanent landscape that does not become overgrown quickly, consider planting slow-growing or dwarf plants. The tradeoff: It may take years before the garden looks mature. On the other hand, if you want to cover an area quickly for screening or shade, you might want to plant fast-growing trees and shrubs. The tradeoff for doing that: Your maintenance costs will rise sharply, and you might have to redesign and replant in a few years.

The Rahn Garden:
Asiatic Influences

This contemporary house, in the northern part of Seattle, sits within a block of Lake Washington. It has narrow, gray vertical-strip wood siding, a feature which landscape architect Keith Geller extended into the garden by wrapping the upper courtyard with a fence of matching pattern and color. Frederick Rahn had lived in Japan for several years, and he decided with Geller to make a landscape reflecting that experience. The result is an upper courtyard and a lower garden that are subtly Japanese in feeling, though they eschew the typical lanterns, bamboo, and stone dipping basin.

You enter the upper courtyard through a gate next to the garage. The fence is topped by a high, doubled rail above and separate from the fence panels themselves. The railing extends over the gate as well. To the right of the gate are a pine and a few granite rocks.

In the courtyard itself, the world changes. Even with the gate open, the driveway and garage disappear because the gateway is set perpendicular to the driveway. All that remains is a small patio of large, square concrete pavers, encircled by plants, rock, and the fence. Because the space is limited, there are only a few trees: a vine maple clump, another pine, and one green-leafed Japanese maple (*Acer palmatum*). With a minimum of pruning, each of these trees can be kept in scale with the courtyard.

The few large stones in the garden are granite. A dry sump area lined with smaller, cobble-sized rock receives the seasonal runoff from the patio and surrounding land. This reflects Geller's philosophy of capturing and using whatever water passes through a yard, rather than dumping it into the next yard downstream. Iris, hostas, and other water-tolerant plants cover the edge of the sump.

Geller planted two very low groundcovers in the area, Corsican mint (*Mentha requienii*) and Scotch moss (*Sagina subulata* 'Aurea'). The Corsican mint is creeping out through the gaps in the pavers, so that anyone who steps on it in passing notices the strong, sweet scent of mint in the air. The easy-care Scotch moss acts as a stand-in for the true mosses that are so revered in Japanese landscaping but which are much harder to maintain.

Other plants in the upper courtyard include a small but old rhododendron 'Moonstone,' which has pale, bell-shaped blossoms and heart-shaped leaves; creeping thrift (*Armeria maritima*), with its chivelike blossoms; variegated deadnettle (*Lamium maculatum*); a deciduous mollis azalea (*Rhododendron* x 'Mollis'); one compact rhododendron 'P.J.M.'; and three very dwarf rhododendrons ('Ramapo,' *impeditum*, and *pemakoense*). The rhodies give a certain amount of color in their season, starting with the very early 'P.J.M.,' but as with most Japanese landscapes, flowers are not the central purpose of this garden. It is meant to be a quiet refuge, not a bandstand.

The lower garden, in the back yard, is again quite small. Fifteen feet out from the basement is a hedge of Castlewellan cypress (x *Cupressocyparis Leylandii* 'Castlewellan'), which the former owner had planted to screen the yard from the busy bicycle trail just below. Geller kept the hedge but removed the flat lawn area and the less-than-flat brick patio, which had settled unevenly over time. He also kept a large plum tree on one side of the yard and a 12-foot-tall lilac clump on the other. In place of the lawn, he installed two berms of soil. The berms are crowned by two plants that Mr. Rahn has been training for several years: a mature red laceleaf Japanese maple (*Acer palmatum* 'Ornatum') and a small, narrow pine.

Below the laceleaf maple is a cobble-lined dry sump that echoes the one in the upper courtyard. Another echo is more Scotch moss, which is used both on the berm and in another raised bed underneath a large raised deck. Plant selection for the lower yard also includes the groundcover kinnikinnick (*Arctostaphylos uva-ursi*) and several uncommon ferns.

The pathway in the lower garden is now made of thick slabs of granite—several tons of it—hauled in by wheelbarrow from the front yard. Their gritty surface is much better for walking on when wet than the glazed brick they replaced. Also, unlike the brick, the granite slabs are set in plenty of sand. They curve out away from the side of the house in a graceful arc,

As with most Japanese landscapes, flowers are not the central purpose of this garden; it is meant to be a quiet refuge, not a bandstand.

rather than first hugging it for a ways and then making a series of right-angle turns. Here, human engineering has won out over the former geometrically rigid pathway that was more suitable for viewing than real use. The granite pavers work their way around to a narrow side yard, where Mr. Rahn keeps some select roses and a planting of *mesclun* (mixed salad greens).

Now, from both the basement window and the deck, you can look out onto a special garden area rather than a small, useless patch of lawn backed by an anonymous hedge.

The Geller Garden:
An Urban Wildlife Sanctuary

Landscape architect Keith Geller's own garden represented entirely different challenges from the Rahn yard. His house sits high above the street in a much older neighborhood on the east side of Capitol Hill in Seattle. Instead of the typical lawn, the parking strip has a wide brick area with cutouts for plant groupings—Shasta daisies (*Chrysanthemum maximum*), green and gray santolinas, and a few Scots pines (*P. sylvestris*). To reach the house, you must climb a long flight of wooden stairs with one landing in the middle to let you catch your breath. Drought-resistant plantings, including yucca and more green and gray santolinas, help to prevent erosion of the hill.

At the top of the stairs, perched next to a wooden gateway, a black wooden crow stands guard. You cannot walk through Keith Geller's yard without seeing birds, both real and artificial. As I took a walk with him through the garden, he would often pause to whistle a call to particular birds in the surrounding trees, and they would reply. The many trees in the yard provide food and shelter for the birds, but they have other purposes as well. The trees are enjoyed for their specific foliage patterns, flowers, and branching structures, and serve as living gates to separate one garden room from another.

Step through the gate, part of a wooden fence that almost encircles the upper portion of the yard, and you notice a hard-to-place fragrance that might remind you of a hope chest. It comes from a piece of wood salvaged from a large nearby Lawson cypress (*Chamaecyparis Lawsoniana*), which split open during a storm one recent winter. The cypress is one of a pair of "dwarf" conifers, now with massive trunks, inherited from a former owner. Geller patched up the wounded cypress, but is not sanguine about its long-term survival. He will be content if it lives until some young Scots pines grow up to replace it. Other trees near the gate include a hawthorn (*Crataegus* sp.) that provides a bounty of fruit for neighborhood wildlife, and a slow-growing alpine fir (*Abies lasiocarpa*).

Walk up a short flight of concrete steps and you are into the next "room," an informal shaded terrace paved and patterned with brick with occasional interruptions of cobbles. In the middle of this terrace are the steps leading to the front porch of the house itself. A *Daphne odora* with cream-edged leaves provides a powerful fragrance when it blooms in late winter. Two brightly painted Adirondack chairs—one yellow, one orange-red—sit to one side. Behind them, a vine maple clump and the other, undamaged Lawson cypress serve as walls closing off the next room. (See cover photo.) This next portion of the garden, on the north side of the house, has a sump area that catches seasonal runoff from the yard. Water-loving plants, including domesticated blueberries, Siberian iris, coltsfoot (*Petasites* sp.), and daylilies, surround this sump, demonstrating the common-sense principle of putting plants where they will best thrive so the homeowner has less work to do.

The path to the back yard proceeds under the shade of a kousa dogwood, vine maples, and two species of styrax, or snowbell (the big-leafed *S. Obassia* and the smaller-leafed *S. japonicus*). When I visited the garden in June, the bark-mulched path was strewn with styrax flowers. Both species have fragrant flowers, although the Obassia snowbell is more noted for its scent. Shade-tolerant plants and flowers, including columbine (*Aquilegia* spp.), shooting star (*Dodecatheon* spp.), numerous ferns, and drifts of native bleeding heart (*Dicentra formosa*), fill the rest of this area.

The side yard to the south is narrow; it borders a city park that has its own wealth of trees. A tall wooden fence separates the yard from the park. Sharp eyes will note the small wooden birdhouse mounted on the side of the fence.

The back yard, on the west side, is split into two areas that receive a good amount of afternoon sun. The upper area has a small patch of lawn—the only lawn on the entire property. The lower area is paved with brick, in the same pattern as in the front. The Adirondack-style furniture on these levels includes an unpainted bench, and chairs painted blue or aqua. The shady side of the lower patio is surrounded with rhododendrons, Japanese anemones, and Pacific wax myrtle (*Myrica californica*), while the sunny west side and the upper area look out onto a perennial garden bordered with a simple two-rail fence. A secluded, grapevine-covered alcove hides beyond the perennial garden in the northwest corner.

The garage in the back yard facing the alley has been converted to an office for Geller's landscape architect practice. Glancing quickly at the pathway between the house and the office, you might think it was made from washed gravel—but walk on it, and you'll realize that it's concrete. Geller took the original walkway, which over time had developed cracks and was unsightly, broke it up, flipped it over, and

◆

The Geller yard's trees are in scale with the house and property; there are no massive oaks or bigleaf maples, no weeping willows or poplars.

◆

mortared it back together upside down, with a few additional cobblestones (which echo others elsewhere in the yard) for decoration. This is a good example of taking stock of a yard and using old materials in new ways.

Unlike some of the spare, lean gardens in this chapter, including the Rahn garden (which Geller designed), Geller's own yard is filled with plants and trees. What makes it manageable is that the trees are in scale with the size of the house and property; there are no massive oaks or bigleaf maples, no holly trees next to pathways, and no weeping willows or poplars. The high percentage of deciduous trees guarantees that there will be cooling shade in the summer and increased light in the winter.

The Withey-Price Garden: Formal and Informal Perennial Beds

The area at the north end of Lake Washington, near Seattle, was once old orchards and farmsteads. Over the last forty to sixty years, pockets of suburbia have crept in, gotten a foothold, and begun to take over. Now, only traces of the older, quieter time remain, side by side with the new. Drive down a short, curved cul-de-sac on a road between Kenmore and Lake Forest Park and you will see a grouping of modern, tidy suburban houses with cedar siding in muted pastel tones. At the end of the cul-de-sac, though, something different happens. From the street you can see an unusual English laurel hedge on one side of a driveway—unusual because it is properly pruned, wider at the base and narrower at the top, so that none of the leaves will get shaded out. On the other side of the driveway is a tall hedge of pyramidalis (*Thuja occidentalis* 'Pyramidalis'). A drift of a low, striped ornamental grass peeks through the foot of this hedge. Between the two hedges you can see a large garage, but no house.

Walk to the top of the driveway and turn to the left, and you will finally see the house. It was built many decades ago, using dark, vertical planks of siding recycled from another project. The house projects an aura of Northwest history, and reminds me of the house not far away in which I grew up. But look to the left, hidden behind the pyramidalis, and you will see the first courtyard. It is formal, European, with an overall rectangle pattern accented by regular groupings of germander, red brick paving, and regularly spaced terra-cotta planters. A solid-wood bench sits to one side. Some of the planting-bed and container residents change seasonally, providing color almost year-round. What humanizes it is a jaunty trailing hydrangea (*Hydrangea anomala petiolaris*) that covers one corner of the house and spills over toward the courtyard. This gives an opening clue to the garden design. The first theme, that of the hedges and the initial courtyard, is one of a formal introduction to the residence. As you move through the garden, the formality is dropped and you can become on more familiar terms with it.

Landscape designers Glenn Withey and Charles Price designed and maintain the half-acre–plus yard, which belongs to Glenn Withey's mother. They use it as a showcase and test garden where they try out different plant combinations, design elements, and horticultural techniques that can eventually be designed into their customers' gardens. I could smell one of these techniques as I circled the home—steer manure, and lots of it. Withey and Price had just finished loading up the garden beds with 30 cubic yards of manure. They do this each spring to replenish the soil in the flower and vegetable gardens, laying it on thickly as a mulch around the emerging plants. It works.

Weed control is mostly done by hand or by crowding. Withey and Price encourage enough healthy growth from the desirable plants that many weeds are out-competed. Because of the sheer volume of herbaceous plants, lawn, and woody shrubs and trees, this yard can be considered high-maintenance. In fact, Withey estimates that during the growing season he and Price average about twenty hours of effort a week in this one yard, including lawn care, transplanting, weeding, occasional pruning, and watering.

But this considerable number of hours could be misleading, since it also includes time the men spend relentlessly tearing out more and more lawn and replacing it with paved patios and larger planting areas. The lawn has disappeared from two sides of the house already. These two sides now look like additional courtyards. The one to the west of the house, below the formal entrance court, begins with a structured look—concrete walls on two sides hidden behind a wooden fascia, with a brick patio. But it opens up on the north side into a curving, crushed gravel path through a large perennial bed, and there are cutouts in the brick where several hostas thrive. The east courtyard, just developed, has a patio of large, pale sandstone squares with a dark circular pool in the center. The east side, too, has a crushed-gravel pathway that curves around through mostly perennial plantings to the lower north part of the yard, which is divided into a lawn area and a vegetable garden below. The vegetable garden has some elements of formality—it is cornered with boxwoods at each terrace level. Withey and Price recently planted dwarf fruit trees along the main path through it. The trees are being arched over curved poles so that they will eventually make a series of fruited arbors down the path. The lower east side of the property, beyond the vegetable garden, is enclosed by hedges of Western red cedar and Leyland cypress (x *Cupressocyparis Leylandii*).

Beyond the eastern courtyard stands a tall hedge of English holly, which hides a garden with many plants of golden- and yellow-hued leaves or flowers. Central to this garden is a golden full-moon maple

(*Acer japonicum* 'Aureum'), with three yellow-leafed locusts (*Robinia pseudoacacia* 'Frisia') acting as guardians. The holly hedge gives a degree of shade to the area, helping to protect the light-colored foliage. Other specialty gardens on the property include a shade garden, with hostas and hellebores, and an alpine garden.

♦

The Withey and Price technique for a grand perennial garden is to divide and conquer: Begin with one area, develop it, and expand to other areas as time allows.

♦

This is certainly an enthusiast's garden. It is designed to give a great deal of joy to gardeners who thrive on working in the yard and who like to experiment. Does this mean that Withey and Price will run out of room to create when all of the lawn has been removed? Not at all. They predict that in two years they will take out most of the perennial plantings and start over with new material. The perennials they remove will wind up in customers' gardens, in friends' gardens, and at plant sales. The yard will hardly be barren, though. All the courtyard structures, hedges, and trees will remain to become the backdrop or foundation for the next design.

If you would like to make a perennial garden as grand as Withey and Price's, you might follow their technique of dividing and conquering: They began with one specific area, developed it, and expanded to additional areas as their time allowed. This is a far saner approach than trying to create such an ambitious garden all at once and burning out in the process.

The Kyper Garden: Drought Tolerance and the Perennial Collector

Rick Kyper is a professional gardener and a perennial enthusiast. His house is in an older urban section of south Seattle, on a ridge between Lake Washington and Puget Sound. Small houses on small lots mingle with larger apartment buildings on the same street. Both the Kyper house and the wall in front of it adjoining the street are faced with brick of a soft golden hue. Concrete steps climb up to and through the center of the wall and merge with a concrete sidewalk that ends in a T of more golden-brick at the front porch steps. The portion of the garden to the left is dominated by a towering evergreen that shelters shade-loving plants beneath. To the right and along the brick wall is a drought-resistant garden; its combination of blues, grays, and yellows works especially well with the color of the nearby brick. Beyond its attractiveness, the garden's water-miserliness allows Kyper to go on extended plant-hunting and garden-viewing expeditions without worrying too much about watering regimens when he is gone.

Maintenance to this garden is relatively low for three reasons: It is small enough that upkeep can be performed quickly; it is planted fully enough that it can choke out most weeds; and the plants are chosen for their drought resistance.

The most frequently used plant in the garden is the green santolina (*S. virens*), which edges both sides of the steps ascending the front wall. Also easy to see as you walk up the stairs is the dainty lady's mantle (*Alchemilla* sp.), which holds drops of water in its leaves on wet or dewy mornings. Neither of these plants is hard to find, and this underscores an important point. The garden strikes a balance between Rick Kyper's two roles as designer and collector. While there are rare plants here—reflecting Kyper's journeys, both in person and through seed and plant catalogs, to nurseries and gardens in England, Ireland, Europe, and beyond—nothing is planted solely because of its rarity.

This dry garden is shaped like a fattened horseshoe, with a short gravel walkway into the center that both serves as a design element and allows easier access to plants in the inner part of the garden. Several varieties of poker plant (*Kniphofia* spp.) send up their flower spikes throughout the summer, mixed with the spikes of delphinium and lilies; cream- and yellow-flowered yarrows (*Achillea* spp.) blend with a bright-golden mint (*Mentha* sp.). Some surprises: a handful of David Austin roses and a Chinese plum yew (*Cephalotaxus Harringtoni*), which are getting by on limited water.

Wintertime brings some decrease in color, but not as much as you might imagine. Although some foliage disappears with the approach of cold, the santolina, plum yew, and some dwarfer groundcovers carry on. A few hours' cleanup in late fall/early winter keeps the garden tidy until spring, when things start popping out again.

The Buckles Garden:
English-American Themes

Susan Buckles has two gardens. One is the grounds of Children's Hospital in Seattle, where she is head gardener. The other surrounds the home she shares with her husband, Alden. Their home garden is a blending of garden themes from her native England and his American background.

The most prominent feature in the front yard is a mature saucer magnolia (*M.* x *Soulangiana*). The Buckleses thinned out its form to a few thick main stems, converting it from an overgrown bush to a shapely midsized tree. This technique gives a far more agreeable result than trying to keep the plant down to shrub size by pinching back the robust tip growth. A pathway of thick, flat stones curves out from the front steps, under the magnolia, toward the street. To balance the large magnolia, Susan and Alden planted an English oak (*Quercus robur*) on the opposite side of the front yard. It will grow at a leisurely rate to great size; even then, it will still be in scale with the house and plantings.

Along the north property line, next to the new oak, runs a cedar split-rail fence designed and built by Alden Buckles. It makes a fine backdrop for the informal planting beds, and lets in a considerable amount of light and air while providing support for some taller plants and vines. The planting scheme is eclectic, with an eye to providing a long season of foliage and flower interest. Trilliums and a primula were blooming the first time I saw the garden; later on came the bush roses and astrantias.

While some gardens reveal everything at once, the Buckles garden rewards close inspection.

A grass pathway, edged with red brick laid flush with the ground, leads to the back yard, where there is a small concrete pond. I first saw the pond on a rainy spring day, and the patterns the raindrops made on the surface of the water reaffirmed my fondness for water. Surrounded by a large rhododendron to the left, an old-fashioned bush rose to the right, a climbing rose on the fence behind, and water-loving perennials at water's edge, the pond is scarcely visible unless you are standing directly in front of it. While some gardens reveal everything at once, this garden rewards close inspection.

Susan Buckles, who lectures on maintaining perennial gardens, emphasizes that consistency of care is important. If you can give your garden a small amount of care each week, then you minimize main-tenance chores. Unlike typical Northwest juniper-and-rhododendron yards, where people might get by only doing spring and fall cleanups, perennial gardens require care whenever the need arises. Ignore weeds until they get a solid foothold, and you may soon feel like abandoning ship. Take a hand trowel or weed grubber with you when you go out to enjoy your flowers. A few hours a week—or even better, a few minutes a day—will keep you in control of your garden's destiny.

The Schieber Garden: Edible Landscaping in an Urban Setting

I had an address in hand when I went to see Gilbert and Carolyn Schieber, but I didn't need it to find their place. Driving slowly down a street of houses fronted with lawn after lawn, I came to a garden that seemed to leap out into the street. Serviceberries (*Amelanchier* spp.) and a plum tree, surrounded by shrubs and perennials, filled the parking strip, and a 10-foot spire of mullein (*Verbascum bombyciferum*) guarded the driveway. In four years, the Schiebers have transformed the plain lawn that covered most of the property into a complex, very personal, and highly productive garden.

The architecture of the house helps to support this horticultural vision. It has dark shingle siding instead of the pale clapboard more typical of the area, so from the outset it presents a different face to the world. There is no longer just a simple concrete front walkway; now, wood-chip pathways wend through raised planting berms. Most of the front yard contains drought-resistant plantings, and the Schiebers do little watering there. They concentrate moisture on productive food plants, most of them in the side and back yards. The south-facing side is covered in part with a "Belgian fence," made up of apple trees closely planted in V-formation instead of upright.

The back yard is divided into several zones, including a duck enclosure, a pond and bog area, and an alpine garden. Wood-chip pathways separate most of these areas. A grouping of tall posts, covered with chicken wire, serves as an enclosure for the three ducks that live in the back yard. They wander freely for much of the day but return to the pen at night; surprisingly, they do not seem to do much damage to the plants. The pond serves both as a bathing spot for the ducks and as an evaporative cooler for the area on hot days.

Although the Schiebers do some hand watering of potted or newly planted material, a close look at their garden reveals two other methods of water delivery. A black polyethylene pipe acts as supply line for a series of spitter-emitters that target plants with high water needs. And at the back side of the house, the downspouts drain to a "bog" area near the pond, where blueberries and other water-loving plants are concentrated.

Besides the apples and blueberries, the Schiebers have also planted kiwi, grapes, tayberry (a blackberry-raspberry hybrid), several species of serviceberry, and lots of alpine strawberries. One grapevine, growing over their garage and greenhouse, can produce over 50 pounds of fruit each year. Although most Northwesterners haven't heard of serviceberries (and grocery stores don't carry them), I suspect that their undemanding culture and mild, sweet flavor could gain favor with a little publicity. People who don't plant trees for fruit might consider planting serviceberries as a lower-maintenance substitute for flowering crabapples—and the fruit can always go to the birds.

Where some gardens sing a simple tune, this garden is polyphonic. The plants are in complex groups according to their climate, care, and soil needs. A certain amount of care each week keeps it in shape. Gil Schieber feels that, for them, it is a low-maintenance yard. By plant enthusiast standards, it is.

The Benedict Garden: Low-Maintenance Roses

It's time we looked at the rose problem head-on. Why does such a beautiful flower come with such an awkward-looking plant? And how do we make roses work in the garden—with the roses doing most of the work, instead of us? One approach, taken by several of the gardens discussed above, is to interplant the roses with lots of perennials to hide the shape of the rosebushes. Another is to use old-fashioned shrub roses, which do make fine-looking bushes but may not bloom as long. A third approach would be to plant only disease-resistant varieties so that we can cut down on the arsenals of insect and disease sprays so many of today's roses require.

Rose fancier Rosann Benedict opted to go with mostly modern roses—about a hundred varieties. She also wanted to keep the visual lines in her garden as simple as possible, which meant that the roses would have to stand on their own, rather than blend in with other plantings. She had a third desire as well, to arrange this extended rose garden to make the expected maintenance as easy as possible.

♦

Rewards of a rose garden: long-stemmed hybrid tea cutting roses from late May through November.

♦

My brother, landscape designer Bill Munro, of Rose Hill Landscaping, worked out a stepped pattern of raised railroad-tie beds for the front and back yards that lifted the rose roots up out of the existing glacial-till soil and put them into decent topsoil. The raised beds, joined by crushed-gravel pathways, allow for easier access to the roses. In addition, they increase air circulation, cutting down on diseases. Bill also designed a group of plants for the periphery of the yard, to give color and shape when the roses are dormant. A large, rare dove tree (*Davidia involucrata*) graces one corner near the street. Nearer the house, a group of compact-growing rhododendron 'Rosa Mundi' and a Royal Purple smoke tree (*Cotinus coggygria*) balance with a vine maple (*Acer circinatum*) and an upright mugho pine (*Pinus mugo*). The familiar blue-flowered *Lithodora diffusa* is paired with a large planting of the uncommon spring-blooming native groundcover *Penstemon Barrettiae*. A nandina (*N. domestica*) and azaleas near the front door round out the front-yard plantings.

Benedict uses a range of materials to keep her roses strong: bone meal, horse manure, fish fertilizer, and epsom salts, in addition to the more typical systemic rose fertilizer/insecticide. She uses a simple aboveground porous-pipe system to irrigate the roses. Because she loves roses and the garden is designed to simplify the necessary tasks, she considers her rose garden to be low-maintenance. Her reward for an hour or two of work per week: long-stemmed hybrid tea cutting roses from late May through November, right outside her door. The rhododendrons stretch the blooming period of her yard back to March and provide a green background to the yard throughout the year.

The Jilka Garden: A Structured Approach

When Dan Jilka bought a house in an older part of the city, he wanted it to fit in with surrounding houses even while he converted it to a professional office. Landscape architect Scott Lankford expanded the scope of the work to include the appearance of the building as well as the landscape itself. The result is a new façade for the house, with a brick patio and raised brick planters that give a unified, refined look to the entire project, yet are in keeping with the era when the neighborhood was built. The planters serve several purposes: They raise all plant material beyond the reach of neighborhood dogs and stray foot traffic; they clearly direct all foot traffic where it is supposed to go, either to the front door of the Jilka house or next door; and, with the L-shaped arbor atop the main planter, they give a partial sense of enclosure without obscuring any line of sight—an important consideration in an urban environment.

Lankford kept the planting scheme restrained, allowing it to fit into the small scale of the yard. There is a mature, upright green-leafed Japanese maple (*Acer palmatum*) on one side and a red laceleaf Japanese maple (*Acer palmatum* 'Ornatum') on the other. A wisteria vine weaves through the open-pattern arbor, which is not connected to the house. (I like this, since I know the mischief wisterias can do if they are allowed to grab onto the siding and roof of a house.) Groundcovers include kinnikinnick (*Arctostaphylos uva-ursi*) and candytuft (*Iberis sempervirens*). A slow-growing mountain laurel (*Kalmia latifolia*) graces one side of the steps to the front porch; beyond it are a group of *Viburnum Davidii* and, for late-summer color, a single hydrangea.

All of this adds up to a very low maintenance yard that looks professional but not institutional. Other than the hydrangea and wisteria, little else needs pruning. There is not much room for invasion by weeds. Only the kalmia might require any special watering consideration.

CHAPTER EIGHT

Site Preparation

Grading, Drainage, Soil, and Irrigation

When you build a house, the first thing that goes in is the foundation. You dig down to solid ground, set up the forms, and pour the concrete. Only then do the walls and roof go up. With landscaping, the same principle holds true, except that the soil is the foundation. It anchors the roots of plants and is their main source for water and nutrients. It is also the underpinning for any walkways, patios, lawns, walls, or fences you might decide to install in your yard.

Clearly, then, it's vital to take care of the ground preparation before you begin planting or constructing your landscape. This is absolutely the best time to work on the grading, drainage, and soil preparation. It's also a good time to think about irrigation—how you are going to get the proper amount of water to your lawn and planting areas. Depending upon your watering needs, you might want to consider installing at least the basic piping for an underground irrigation system before planting the shrubbery; if you wait until the plantings are done, you could face extra expense and a major disruption of plants.

It's also not too soon to think about mulches when preparing the site for landscaping. If your budget or schedule prevents you from preparing your soil or planting everything on your plan immediately, a mulch could help you control erosion and hold off the onslaught of weeds until you're ready.

Grading

You may want to change the grade in your yard for aesthetic reasons, practical reasons, or both. Flat or gently sloping spaces are usable spaces. Steep slopes make visually dramatic spaces—and make for dramatic problems as well. It is difficult and dangerous to mow a sloping lawn, for instance. It is much harder to navigate on slopes too; pushing a wheelbarrow, setting up a lawn chair, or even just walking around the yard can be challenging. Maintenance of flower beds, shrubs, and trees is harder. Watering hillsides effectively is also more difficult because the water tends to run off rather than be absorbed into the soil—and the runoff is apt to carry soil with it.

But I am not going to suggest that you grade out every spot in your yard to the same level. That may not be possible, especially if you have a great difference in elevation from one corner of your yard to another. And a perfectly flat yard can be visually uninteresting. At the very least, though, you should determine how foot and equipment traffic will move through your yard; then you can adjust the grade to make it flow smoothly.

One effective solution is to terrace the land. Terracing has been used for centuries in Asia, Europe, and Africa—wherever people who live in hilly regions need to get the most use out of the land yet not have their soil wash away in the rainy season. In your garden you can create level areas by building retaining walls of rock, timbers, or concrete, and then linking the higher and lower areas with steps or ramps made of similar materials. It often makes more

◆

It's vital to take care of the ground preparation before you begin planting or constructing your landscape.

◆

sense to have more levels and with lower walls, than fewer levels with bigger changes of elevation and higher walls. Lower walls allow for the use of smaller rocks, for instance, which means they are more suitable for do-it-yourself landscapers. In Chapter 9, "Construction Techniques," we'll go into more detail about retaining walls.

If you do decide to do major sculpting of the grade in your yard, your first step should be to examine the top layer of soil you intend to move. In most undisturbed areas, there will be a layer of reasonably good topsoil—probably not as good as you might purchase from a topsoil supplier, but decent enough and definitely cheap. It might be from a few inches to a foot deep. Below that, you will see progressively

less desirable layers, ending with clay or hardpan (extremely dense, compacted soil)—or worse yet, solid rock.

Traditional wisdom suggests that you scrape off the native topsoil and set it aside before you reshape the ground, and then redistribute the topsoil back over the land when the grading is done. Unfortunately, you are not likely to have an undisturbed soil profile in your yard. All too typically, construction practices dictate expediency. When a hole is dug for a house foundation, the subsoil that is removed will quite likely be used to do fill grading and final grading around the house. The resulting soil profile is likely to be a hodgepodge, with disturbed subsoil on top of what little topsoil might be left.

Grading to increase useful space. Note the gentle sloping away from the house; the upper terracing with timber planters to contain soil on the slope; the berm in the lower yard to help raise plant roots above a section of water-soaked soil.

Some builders, if they see stretches of good soil in a subdivision, may sell it off to recoup some of their development costs—in which case you could conceivably end up buying back your own soil from a topsoil company. If your yard's topsoil is gone or has been contaminated with subsoil, then trying to save the existing topsoil will be a wasted effort.

What if your problem is not a hilly site, but a totally flat one? One effective trick for livening up this kind of terrain is to create a few strategic low berms, or mounds of soil, here and there about the property. The key words are "low" and "few." A supple swell is far more effective than an imitation burial mound. Use the berms as centerpieces to show off plantings of favorite plants and trees. Connect higher and lower mounds together to give the impression of a grouping of hills.

A more formal means of creating height contrast, and one that is very useful in some landscape contexts, is to build raised beds of various levels, using timbers, rocks, or other supporting materials. Either method, berms or raised beds, has the advantage of raising plant roots above the former soil level, which is important if your existing soil drains poorly. The raised areas help with traffic control too. Combined with well-defined pathways, they can direct traffic around, rather than across, planting areas—although pets and some children may not get the hint.

Raised decks and other structures can also add interest to flat yards. Although decks typically adjoin houses, they can also be placed away from the house, connected only by a walkway or bridge. As a simple exercise, take a footstool or a small stand-alone ladder around to various places in your yard. From a vantage point of one, two, or three feet off the ground, look for a place with a particularly pleasing view, with the right mix of sun and shade or the right degree of privacy. (If you haven't yet planted any of the trees that will supply the desired shade, you may have to do some creative imagining.)

One last word about flat land. Totally flat ground can flood when the soil reaches its saturation point. If you get pools of standing water in your yard when it rains, that's all the more reason for adjusting the slope. Gentle slopes, just a few degrees away from level, allow a good degree of water absorption but have the ability to slough off excess water. Although it's not always possible, ideally you should strive to grade your yard so that it slopes away from your house in all directions.

Raised beds or berms lift plants above the former soil level, aiding drainage and helping control traffic in the yard.

Grading Equipment

If you have had experience with power grading equipment, you may be able to do the actual grading yourself. If you have never climbed onto a grader, loader, or tractor, I don't recommend that you learn how to operate one now, especially if you live on a hillside. Even professional landscapers make mistakes with this kind of equipment. State departments of labor and industry show an awareness of this by setting their risk rates for landscapers based upon claims experience.

Many of the smaller vehicles, such as those you find at typical consumer rental shops, are amazingly easy to tip over, and they lack the power to cut through harder soils quickly. They are most useful for maneuvering in tight corners where bigger machines can't tread, in small yards with no hills, and in places where the soil is too soft or fragile for larger machinery. (Heavy bulldozers are notorious for compacting soils, reducing vital air and water permeability, and damaging existing tree roots.)

One of the most practical types of small equipment is a rubber-tired tractor with a scoop on the front and a tiller on the back. These tractors are especially popular with professional landscapers, who appreciate their adaptability. For yards with softer soils, you can often use the turned blade of the scoop to do minor grading; with some tiller attachments,

One of the most practical types of small equipment is a rubber-tired tractor with a scoop on the front and a tiller on the back.

you can flip over the tiller mechanism and use it as a drag float for further grading. You can also use the tiller to help break up harder soils to make the grading easier, or to move topsoil around the yard and then till the new soil in with the existing soil. Tractors are also useful for lifting or dragging heavy objects— big plants, rocks, timbers.

One thing tractors can't do very well is dig tidy, effective ditches. For that you will need either a trenching machine or a backhoe-loader. Trenching machines often look like oversized chain saws with wheels. Depending upon their size, they can dig anything from narrow slit trenches for irrigation pipes or outdoor wiring to wide trenches for wall footings or drainage gravel and pipe.

The larger machines from big-equipment rental shops are effective, but quite costly. Each type of machine has its own particular uses.

◆ The rubber-tired loader with a big scoop is useful for minor grading, but even more useful for scooping and hauling large quantities of loose soil and other materials. Its rubber tires allow it to travel on pavement without scarring although, fully loaded, it can crack the edges of any concrete driveway or walkway that is built over unstable ground.

◆ The traditional bulldozer-grader with a flat front blade can cut inexorably at the hardest soils. The blade will not pick up soil, but it can be manipulated. The left and right sides of the blade can be angled forward or up and down, allowing the blade to remain horizontal even though the dozer is riding at an angle.

- ◆ The tractor-loader with a combination bucket and blade up front is my favorite. Configured as a bucket, it allows you to scoop up loose soil like a loader. You can also flip the jaws of the bucket open and use the exposed flat blade much as you would the blade of a grader, although you cannot raise the left or right side of the blade separately. Because the bucket can articulate out away from the blade, you can also use the front end to grasp objects that you cannot easily scoop up: stumps, roots, large rocks. Be careful how tightly you hold on to things, though. If you should spring the bucket so that its parts no longer line up correctly, you will have to pay for repairs. Metal-bucket orthodontia can be as expensive as its human equivalent.

If you have driven only cars or light trucks, take note that the controls for braking, accelerating, and turning are quite different on most big earthmovers, graders, and loaders. Don't expect to be an instant expert with the controls. Before you decide to rent anything, get an estimate from at least one licensed, bonded grading service. Although the hourly rate for a machine with an operator will be higher than the rate for the machine alone, an experienced operator should be able to finish the job much faster than an inexperienced one. Overall, then, it might be cheaper

to hire than rent — and it could be a lot safer too. In either case, reread the section on avoiding obstacles in Chapter 2, "Visualization," and be sure to

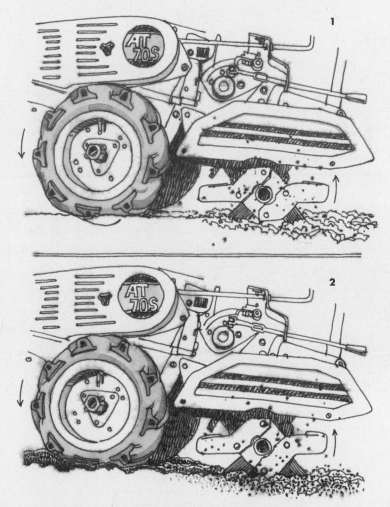

1. Till one time before you add topsoil or soil amendment.
2. Add topsoil or soil amendment and till again.

locate your underground utilities before you start scraping. Remember the aboveground wiring in your yard, too: Raised buckets make excellent wire-catchers.

Drainage

There are ways we can control and use water in our yards without causing negative effects for ourselves or the neighbors.

Water can come to your yard in several ways: directly from rain; from surface runoff from your roof, driveway, or street; from sprinkler systems and hoses; from streams and aquifers crossing your yard; or from your uphill neighbors. You want some water to pass through your soil—to come, linger long enough to help the growing things in the yard, and then depart gracefully, without too much coaxing and without stealing your soil away. What you need are methods to help you hold enough water in the soil for your own uses and to get rid of excess water. Water becomes a problem when it settles in low spots in your yard, turning soil muddy, drowning your plants, perhaps flooding your basement or the crawl space beneath your house. This is a neat balancing act, indeed.

The all-too-common way to deal with excess water, and the one that is the despair of your surface-water management utility, is to catch any loose surface water you can find on your property and dump it, boldly or surreptitiously, into public storm sewers, out onto the street, or into your downhill neighbor's yard. Unfortunately, this method has some side effects.

Picture the soil and plant life in your neighborhood when it was wilderness as a huge sponge. When rain fell, a little drained off, but a lot more was absorbed by vegetation or soaked into the ground, where it was stored and only gradually passed along in evaporation and subsoil water flow. Now, picture this sponge stripped of its greenery and covered with large amounts of asphalt and concrete, and watch what happens. Rainfall produces lots of surface runoff, and very little absorption. As the end result of all the manmade surfacing and housing, we see pictures on the evening news of record flooding in the lowlands, with cows and houses floating downstream.

I don't recommend that you try to catch all incoming water and trap it on your property if you live on a steep hillside with unstable or questionable soil. That could be the perfect method to push your house loose from its moorings and float it downhill on a cushion of mud. But there are some ways most of us can control and use water in our yards without causing negative side effects for ourselves or the neighbors. These could include proper grading (discussed above), a drainage system, and mulches (discussed toward chapter's end).

DRAINAGE PIPES: Drainage pipes are useful for intercepting and redirecting water. The standard pipe in use is ADS plastic corrugated tile. The corrugations give it an accordionlike appearance and also add considerable structural strength. Once it is properly installed in the ground, it is hard to damage. It's flexible, which makes it useful for snaking around obstructions when you are laying the pipe. It is typically 4 inches in diameter (although you might also see 3-inch- and 6-inch-diameter pipe) and comes in 10-foot lengths or in 100- or 200-foot rolls.

The ADS pipe can be either perforated or tight-line. The perforated pipe has many small slits or holes around its circumference. This allows water to seep into it (and out of it), which makes it useful for pulling water out of one place and dispersing it else-where over a broad area. If you are getting water into your yard from the uphill side, you can put a line of perforated pipe across the face of the oncoming water and then direct the water to a more convenient place in the yard—into a planting bed, for instance, and away from lawns and sidewalks.

Tight-line pipe is useful primarily for capturing water at one end and transporting it some distance away. It is especially useful for attaching to down-spouts so that you can get your rooftop water away from the foundation of your house. Also, you can link perforated and tight-line pipe. For example, you might attach 10 feet or more of tight-line to your downspouts and then snake perforated pipe out to wherever you want the water to go.

Forty years ago, concrete drain tiles were the

disperse here

capture here

perforated

tight-line

Drainage profile. Use tight-line drainage tile near downspouts, and perforated tile surrounded by gravel to capture water and disperse it elsewhere, over a broad area.

standard. They lasted a long time in the ground because they didn't rust or rot. Laid into a ditch and surrounded by washed drainage gravel to encourage the flow of water, they were essentially indestructible. Their disadvantage was that they constantly silted up; dirt and mud filtered into the surrounding drainage gravel, crept into the connections between the tiles, and plugged everything up. Sometimes tree roots would push at the tiles so that they became misaligned; the roots could then grow into the tiles and contribute to the blockage. After a certain number of years, the tiles became more archaeological artifact than useful tool. Either you dug up the tile and reinstalled it with new gravel, or your drainage system failed to do its work.

Many shortcomings of concrete tiles are avoided with ADS pipe, which can flex around tree roots and minimize invasive mud and dirt.

Many of the shortcomings of concrete tiles can be avoided by using ADS pipe, especially if you use the longer lengths. Tree roots are less likely to misalign the pipe because it can flex around the roots as they grow. Dirt and mud are less likely to filter into the pipe—although some will still manage to get inside. You also still run the risk of plugging up the system when dirt sifts into the surrounding gravel. There are ways to minimize this; they will add to the expense when you first install the drainage system, but will help to keep the tile useful much longer.

Start with a normal-sized drainage ditch, at least a foot deep and a foot across. Lay enough drainage fabric into the ditch to fill the bottom, come up the sides, and fold back over the top. Dupont Mirafi™ is one brand name for this fabric; it allows water to seep through but holds back the soil. Although the material is very strong, it can be cut to shape with regular scissors. Like most other plastics (including the ADS drain tile) that are not in direct contact with sunlight, it has a very long lifespan.

Although the traditional material for drainage-ditch use is ⅞-inch and 1½-inch washed gravel, I like to use pea gravel instead because it is easier to handle and works about as well. Put the pipe and gravel into the ditch, and wrap the top flaps of the fabric over the top of the gravel. You can then cover the ditch with river rock or a thin layer of bark mulch. Some contractors use a variation on this theme: ADS pipe that is prewrapped with a drainage fabric. Although it won't prevent the gravel from silting up, it will keep the pipe itself free-flowing. If you use this type, be gentle with the pipe wrapping; it is not as sturdy as the rolls of fabric.

Drainage fabric has other uses too. If you want to use plants that must have a loose, fast-draining soil, you can lay the fabric beneath berms of the looser soil to keep it separated from areas of swamp soil underneath. Don't put this material beneath trees, though; their roots can't penetrate it, so the trees can't anchor themselves properly. (For more on root anchoring, see the section on soil preparation below. For a description of other uses of drainage fabric, see the section on paths and patios in Chapter 9, "Construction Techniques.")

Soil Preparation

Where your plants are concerned, there is no such thing as generic dirt. Dirt is what you walk on but otherwise ignore. Soil is what plants and trees grow in—if they can. What all plants share is a need for the four-legged stool of soil quality: air permeability, water retention, an anchoring structure, and the ability to hold and release nutrients upon demand. Where plants differ is in how those requirements are balanced. Water-loving plants need a soil that holds water, while water-hating plants need a quick-draining soil.

It is astonishing that such a variety of familiar and rare garden plants can, with little help from people, survive in the wide range of soils they find in the Northwest. This is what allows us to place plants that need acid soils, such as rhododendrons, azaleas, and camellias, near alkali-loving plants, such as lilacs. Good taste aside, it also allows yucca and other desert plants to survive near swamp cypress and dainty alpine gems. It allows us to throw lawn seed or sod upon inappropriate, barren soil and expect some sort of greenery to result. Still, it's

wisest to pay attention to the soil needs of plants if we want to obtain optimum results from our investment.

The best time to improve the soil in your yard is before you plant anything. Once you start planting, your options begin to evaporate. You might consider hiring a soils expert to help you pinpoint exactly how to improve the soils in different spots around the yard. This costs money, but you end up with an accurate assessment of how good your soil quality is, and where and how to improve it. The soils expert should be able to evaluate the different components of your soil's fertility, including major nutrients such as nitrogen, phosphorus, and potassium as well as minor nutrients; to determine how well the soil percolates, or drains; and to assess its level of organic matter, or humus.

There are also some quick, inexpensive tests you can do to get a first impression of your soil quality. The packaged soil-testing kits that you can buy at nurseries and garden centers have a certain limited usefulness. You will need to read the instructions to determine what a particular test can reveal about soil fertility: Does it measure nutrients? Which ones? Does it measure soil acidity?

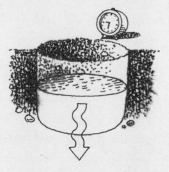

Testing for soil permeability.

There is another quick test, this time for drainage. Dig a number of percolation holes in the soil around your house. The holes should be at least a foot deep and about a foot across. Fill each hole with water and see how long it takes to drain. If the hole takes an hour or longer to drain, the soil in that spot holds too much water. If it drains within five minutes or so, the soil drains too quickly. This test will also help guide you in your choice of soil amendments (discussed below). If you want to plant in a slow-draining area, you will have to do one or more of the following: install a drainage system, as described above; use water-loving plants; or put in raised beds or berms of topsoil to keep roots out of the wetter soil.

Next, take a look at your soil texture. Percolation ability is closely tied to texture. Fast-draining soils usually have a high gravel or sand content. The sand particles are large, as soil particles go, and not much can cling to them—not much water, not much nutrient content. Straight sand or gravel has excellent air permeability, though. Except for those areas of your yard where you're trying to smooth out a section for planting a lawn, don't fret much about gravel in your soil. You could do worse. Clay is worse. It holds vast amounts of water in its tiny particles and allows very little air circulation. Other than horsetail and a few other intrepid weeds, few plants actually thrive in high-clay soils. Silt is between sand and clay in particle size. If it is not too compacted, it will allow some air circulation, yet still hold a fair amount of water.

In real life, there aren't many examples of "pure" soil types. What we mostly see are called "aggregates"—sand blended with silt (sandy loam), or silt blended with clay (clay loam). And, preferably, any of these mixtures should be blended with organic matter.

Some years ago, I ran across a gag-gift digital calculator. It was a piece of solid plastic with five fingerholes. Ask it any mathematical question, and the answer was always 5. Problem soils are like that; no matter what the problem, adding organic material is likely to help. It will slow down water movement in sandy soils, and it will increase air circulation in denser soils. The material could be finely ground sawdust or bark mulch, manure, topsoil mix, or one of the commercial composts made from composted sludge or (more recently) yard waste.

Organic material is *not* a cure-all. It will not magically balance every nutritional shortcoming of your soil. It is, however, a useful tool for improving the tilth, or cultivated condition, of the soil. For a detailed analysis of soil-quality issues in the Pacific Northwest, by all means read Steve Solomon's *Growing Vegetables West of the Cascades* (Sasquatch Books, 1989). Many of his comments apply to gardens east of the mountains too.

Plain sawdust is one of the cheapest organic materials. It works very well for amending extremely large areas on a tight budget, provided you add some form of nitrogen and mix the nitrogen-bearing material in evenly. If you don't enrich the sawdust with nitrogen (or buy it pre-enriched), it will rob available nitrogen from the surrounding soil particles to help it decompose. Plants placed in nitrogen-poor soil will show yellowish leaves and stunted growth. Spread about 3 to 4 pounds of high-nitrogen fertilizer (ammonium sulfate or ammonium nitrate) for each cubic yard of sawdust.

Bark mulch is more expensive than sawdust, but it is another wonderful soil amendment when supplemented with nitrogen. Most bark sold in the Northwest comes from Douglas fir or Western hemlock. One bark or sawdust I would avoid is Western red cedar, which in large quantities is toxic to some plants—but you'll rarely find any at your local bark supply yard. Why use bark as an amendment if other materials are available for less? Because you can spread bark initially as a mulch over areas you won't have time to develop for a while, and then till it in when you're ready to proceed. Even if you leave it undisturbed, it will improve the soil below as it decays and leaches downward.

Chippings, created by pruning services when they prune or fell trees, are a variation on this theme. Most tree services have chippers that turn small-diameter branches and twigs into a very serviceable mulch (the finer the grind, the better the mulch). They often need a convenient place to dump their grindings before going on to the next pruning job. If your yard is in their line of travel, their bounty may cost you nothing at all. Ask beforehand whether the wood chips contain a high percentage of Western red cedar. As with sawdust and bark, you will have to add nitrogen. You can also buy or rent a chipper to chop up material you prune yourself.

Why bother using a soil amendment that needs to have nutrients added to it before it can grow plants successfully? Because by doing so you improve the soil structure, which is at least as important as the soil fertility. And anyway, most of the nutrients you add in now to help decompose the organic material will be available to plants when the decomposition is complete.

Two recycled products that already contain considerable nitrogen and are available for moderate cost are manure and commercial compost. Manure from cows or chickens is the most popular around here, and either works well. Homemade compost is also a wonderful soil amendment, but we usually don't have anywhere near enough of a quantity, right at the beginning, to incorporate it into our soil. The commercial composts may be made either from composted sewage sludge, salvaged from our sewage treatment plants, or from

◆

Bark is an excellent soil amendment, spread initially as a mulch over areas you won't develop for a while, then tilled in when you're ready to proceed.

◆

collected yard waste, including lawn clippings, chipped tree branches, leaves, and shrub prunings. Do you feel uncomfortable at the thought of using sludge in your yard? It is tested for pathogenic organisms and heavy-metal contamination before being released, and should be safe for most purposes—although suppliers will suggest that you use it in non-food-producing, ornamental plantings. For the same reason of caution, I prefer to use recycled yard waste only in ornamental areas too, since I have no control over what garden chemicals the former owners of the clippings used.

If you use peat moss as a soil amendment, look for the rough-textured variety, which is preferable to the very fine type popularly sold.

Baled peat moss is the most expensive of silt soil amendments. It's cost-effective only if you need a very small amount, or if your planting area is inaccessible by wheelbarrow or truck, such as a raised deck or a third-floor condominium balcony. When you calculate how many cubic yards of organic material you need to amend your soil, and realize that it takes nearly seven 4-cubic-foot bales to make a single cubic yard, it doesn't make economic sense to use peat moss to prepare a large landscape area.

If you do decide to use peat moss as a soil amendment, look for the rough-textured variety, which is preferable to the almost–powder-fine bales most places sell. (You can use fine-textured peat as well, though it is more suitable as a top-dressing for lawn preparation.) You may have to ask around for the rough-grind peat at several nurseries, or special-order it from your local nursery, but doing so can be worth the effort; it helps to break up hard soils better than the fine peat. I don't recommend using peat moss by itself as a planting medium. It's so lightweight when it dries that it doesn't serve as a very good anchor. It's also difficult to make wet again once it dries out, since water tends to bead up and roll away rather than be absorbed down into it.

You can also buy pre-mixed topsoil. Many topsoil and bark companies have both standard and custom mixes; some will customize orders of 20 cubic yards or more, with amendments tailored to your specific needs. If you have a special mix you prefer, call around for prices.

SOIL AMENDMENT QUANTITIES: Let's say, as an example, that you want to prepare a planting area of 1000 square feet (20 by 50 feet; 1000 isn't much), and you've estimated that you need to add about 6 inches of soil amendment over the entire area, mixed in with the top 12 inches of existing soil, to give you an overall organic content of 33%. This is typical practice for many landscapers, though your specific needs may vary from zero to much more than that. One cubic yard (27 cubic feet) would cover 54 square feet of area 6 inches deep. Nineteen cubic yards would cover 1026 feet of area 6 inches deep, or 2052 square feet 3 inches deep. These kinds of calculations show how useful it is to determine beforehand how much amending—and what kind—you actually need to do.

I prefer to till the area first, before adding the amendment, and then till the area again after the amendment has been spread about evenly. This double-tilling incorporates the new soil into the old much better. (A large tractor does the job much more effectively than a small hand-tiller. Hand-turning with a good spade can also work well, but it takes a lot more time and effort. Some sturdy gardeners believe that hand-tilling disturbs the tilth of the soil less than mechanical tilling does. You might be able to use the tractor to scoop up and move the amendment into place too.) I absolutely do not recommend just dumping a thin layer of soil amendment or topsoil on top of existing soil when preparing for new plantings. You risk what is called the soil-interface effect, where roots grow down only through the first stratum of good soil and then grow sideways, instead of penetrating into the soil below. Shallow-rooted plants and trees are the first to suffer from drought in dry times, and the first to tip over during windstorms.

IMPROVING SOILS IN EXISTING PLANTINGS: Not all of us move into a new house with a bare yard. If you've inherited existing plants, it becomes more complicated, but not impossible, to help fix soil quality. In this case, your best option is to pinpoint the plants that need the most help. You can help either by digging up these selected plants, mixing in generous amounts of soil amendment, and replanting, or by periodic top-dressing with some of the amendment. As I mentioned above, mixing the soil is best, but some of the nutrients and organic material in the top-dressing will eventually leach down into the existing soil and help the plants. Be careful not to suffocate your plants by piling up ever-higher layers of soil amendment around their trunks, and you will be helping your plants to do their best.

CONTROLLING COSTS: Amending soil costs money and takes time. But what if you don't have much of either? You can still have a good-looking garden if you choose your plantings to fit the existing situation, rather than adjusting the soil to match the needs of the plants you've selected. This means choosing plants that will tolerate, or even thrive in, whatever soil you already have. The list of suitable plants will be smaller but could still be substantial. One possibility you could pursue is plants with nitrogen-fixing roots, including many members of the pea family (Leguminosae), such as the cultivated brooms (*Genista* spp.) and locust (*Robinia* spp.). I'm not fond of our native red alder (*Alnus rubra*) because caterpillars love it so much, but it is a nitrogen-fixing plant that thrives just about anywhere. Other plants and trees native to your specific area could be good candidates—see the "Native Plants" listing in the Appendix. For extensive lists of plants adapted to specific soil acidity ranges, look for the dictionary entry on soils in *Hortus Third*, Liberty Hyde Bailey Hortorium (Macmillan Publishing Co, 1976).

Irrigation

Whether you are creating a new garden or renovating an old one, I encourage you to install an irrigation system—even if you're on a tight budget. The value of your plantings will far outweigh the cost of your irrigation system, and a watering system will help to keep your plantings valuable. To me, the system is not an expense, but an investment with a generous payback.

If you live on the rainy side of the Cascades, you might not feel that an irrigation system should be high on your list of priorities. Most of us are better off for having one, though. You really can't rely upon

Simplified view of an overlapping three-zone sprinkler system, designed for controlling plant losses during times of drought: 1. Lawn area—highly expendable. 2. Annuals and perennials or drought-resistant plants—small-area spray heads. 3. Drip irrigation for valuable plants that will need help in dry times.

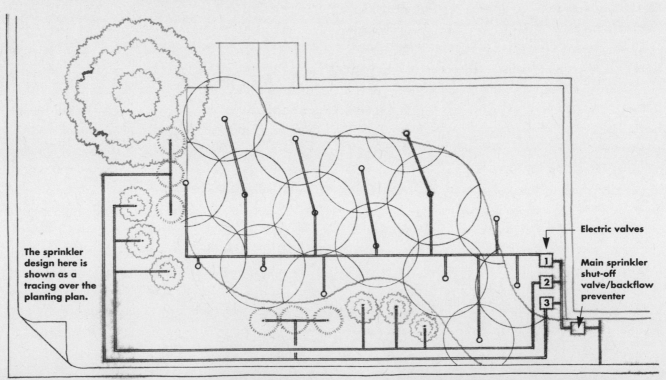

The sprinkler design here is shown as a tracing over the planting plan.

Electric valves

Main sprinkler shut-off valve/backflow preventer

1

2

3

the rain falling when your plants need it—witness a recent summer when the Puget Sound region had 46 consecutive days without rain. Even plants that are drought-resistant will benefit from supplemental waterings, especially during the first few years until they get established. Or you might think that you can do all the necessary watering yourself. If so, we'd better look at what you'll have to do very soon if you don't install an irrigation system.

The most labor-intensive way to deliver water to your plants is to drag a hose around and spray each plant. You can see this ritual enacted in yards everywhere, usually on weekends or in the evening when people get home from work. The second most labor-intensive way is to drag a hose with a sprinkler around from area to area and let the sprinkler run in each place for a while.

With the above methods, the plants must rely upon natural rainfall and human schedules for the amount of water they get and when (or whether) they get it. Few people have enough time, at the right time, to water correctly. If other duties keep you from watering when the plants need water, the plants will suffer.

IRRIGATION SYSTEM PLACEMENT: Once you decide to put in a watering system, you'll need to figure out whether to place it above or below ground level. I prefer underground irrigation systems for aesthetic and practical purposes. All the piping and wiring is underground; once they are in the ground, they're essentially invisible to the casual eye. They are also less susceptible to damage from foot traffic and frost than on-the-surface systems that you attach to hose bibbs. But going underground will cost more money and take a lot more work to accomplish, and an aboveground system can be both affordable and effective. In the pages below, we'll discuss both methods of getting water to your plants.

When you have determined which type (or types) of system best suits your yard's needs, you will need to put together a system design and make up a parts list. It will help immensely if you draw the plan to the same scale as your planting plan, since you will want to coordinate the system to deliver water to where the plants go.

PRELIMINARY STEPS: Designing and installing an effective sprinkler system takes study and skill, but it's not a daunting process if you do it a step at a time. Start your planning with a simple, nondestructive test to measure how fast your pipes can deliver water. Get a 5-gallon bucket, turn on an outside faucet full force, and swing the bucket under the flow of water. Time how long it takes to fill the bucket. Divide that time into 60 and multiply the result by 5 to get your gallons-per-minute rating. If the bucket takes 10 seconds to fill, then your pipes can deliver (60 ÷ 10) x 5, or 30 gallons per minute.

Since most water delivery devices (sprinklers,

spray heads, and the like) are rated in gallons per minute, this will give you a good idea of how many devices you can put onto one sprinkler line or zone. If your water system can deliver 20 gallons of water per minute, and you want to install sprinkler heads rated at 2 gallons per minute each, then you could theoretically place 10 of those heads on one line. In real life, you would want to use fewer than that, because backflow preventers, valves, and even the pipe itself will steal a bit of water pressure. Conversely, if your system can deliver 40 gallons per minute, and you want only 10 sprinkler heads rated at 2 gallons per minute each on a given line, you will need a pressure-reducing device so that you don't overburden the heads; too much pressure could result in unpredictable spray patterns. I suggest you don't mix different types of sprinkler devices on the same zone—it makes it harder to gauge water delivery.

Detail of pop-up sprinkler assembly hidden in the ground.

DELIVERY METHODS: There are many different ways to get water to the plants. Each has its advantages for a specific purpose, but some are clear winners for home landscapers. Most of them are suitable for both aboveground and underground irrigation systems. All of these methods will benefit from the use of dirt screens—mesh inserts designed to keep dirt or other debris from clogging up the outlets.

- The traditional impulse-head sprinkler has a mechanical arm that clacks around in a full or partial circle. Some of these are rigid aboveground fixtures; others rest in hidden pop-up canisters. The pop-ups are better protected against young children, vandals, and carelessness. They are most useful for areas covered primarily with one type of vegetation—a groundcover bed or a level lawn, for instance, where taller vegetation doesn't obstruct the sprinkler head's line of spray.

  Advantages: These sprinklers can water a large radius of ground at once, so you need fewer devices to cover an area. Large droplets don't evaporate into the air as much as water from a misting sprinkler. Clogged orifices and broken mechanical parts are only very occasional problems.

  Disadvantages: They paint with a very broad brush. All plants and all bare ground within reach, regardless of water needs, get the same amount of water. The larger water particles can cause more soil compaction than fine misters. And what does touch land is more likely than smaller drops to run off, causing erosion and wasting water.

- Spray heads come in a range of designs that emit anything from fine sprays to rotating streamers of water.

  Advantages: They allow increased flexibility of placement. You can cover a smaller group of plants, or an irregularly shaped garden area, by careful placement of heads. Spray heads work well in a "zoned" sprinkler system design (see the section below on the parts of the sprinkler system). And they are gentler on the soil than impulse or (worse yet) oscillating sprinklers.

Disadvantages: They clog occasionally. There is some evaporation, and their coverage is uneven on windy days. The more complex network requires more maintenance.

- Recycled-rubber soaker hoses and water-permeable plastic tubing work well for ground-level delivery. Even cheap plastic soaker hoses can be used to good effect, but the recycled rubber and the semi-rigid tubing will last far longer and give a gentler flow of water.

Advantages: These materials can be buried just under the surface so that all the water is delivered to the soil and none is lost to surface runoff or evaporation. They make excellent sense for confined areas, such as raised vegetable beds; for narrow planting beds or strips; or for areas where plants are changed on a regular or seasonal basis.

Disadvantages: This kind of system works best on level ground. On hills, the water will come out more strongly from the lower regions of the pipe. You will also have to take extra steps to determine whether a given area is getting sufficient coverage, since you won't be able to see directly the results of watering. Algae buildup can clog the pores of the plastic tubing; vendors of some permeable tubing suggest that you flush it with a chlorine bleach solution once or twice a year. This buildup is not a problem with rubber products, which have larger pores.

- Micro-spray heads, spitter-emitters, and drip irrigation work with small-gauge "spaghetti" tubing plugged into larger polyethylene tubing.

Advantages: These devices can supply water with pin-point accuracy to yard plantings, and they are also perfect for delivering water to deck or patio flower-pots or to hanging baskets. As watering needs change, you can add or subtract individual devices to suit. Some of the micro-spray heads allow you to individually adjust their water flow.

Disadvantages: The number of parts increases system complexity. This will be especially evident if little feet or fingers go through your planting beds, pulling up connections by accident or out of curios-ity. You will need to examine each outlet on a regu-lar basis to make sure that it's still plugged in and not clogged. I recommend that you use at least $\frac{3}{16}$-inch end-delivery tubing to minimize clogging. Many commercial growers of container plants swear by drip irrigation because it puts water only where it will do good. When a given plant is sold, they simply pop another container into the same spot, or cap off the individual pipe.

A SIMPLE ABOVEGROUND SYSTEM: An aboveground system is not quite as convenient as a fully automatic system, but it's a step in the right direction, and is well within the ability of any do-it-yourselfer. It is made up of simple components, and takes less skill to install than an underground system. It should require no electrical and scant plumbing experience to install. While any watering system should be thought out beforehand, the plan for an aboveground system can be much more casual. How permanent is an above-ground irrigation system? I installed my first simple drip irrigation system over a decade ago, and it's still working with minimal maintenance.

An aboveground irrigation system is well within the ability of any do-it-yourselfer.

Aboveground watering systems are usually hooked onto a hose bibb instead of directly into your house's main water supply. A typical configuration consists of an anti-siphon device hooked to the hose bibb, followed by a wind-up metering valve, flexible black polyethylene pipe to get the water to the planting area, and porous pipe or small-volume sprinklers or emitters (described above) to do the actual water delivery. The metering device must be wound up by hand; it delivers the amount of water that you have indicated (usually expressed in gallons) and then shuts itself off. It won't automatically turn itself back on. For more money, battery-powered timer valves are available that will cycle the system on and off automatically.

AN UNDERGROUND IRRIGATION SYSTEM: In addition to the actual output devices (sprinklers, porous pipes, or drippers), the following elements are common to most types of underground automatic sprinkler systems:

♦ A backflow-prevention device. Depending upon the requirements of your local water utility, this could be a vacuum breaker, a double-check valve, or a double-check valve with a reduced-pressure device. A backflow-prevention device keeps sprinkler water from backing up into and contaminating the general water supply. It is critical that you learn and follow the local regulations. We take safe water for granted, but it happens only because so many people work hard to keep it that way.

♦ A main shut-off valve. This is usually connected directly to the main water line coming into the house.

♦ An electric timing and control device. This allows you to water your yard automatically. More important, it allows you to deliver different amounts of water to different sections, or "zones," of the yard. It makes sense to group plants with similar water needs together. Put high-water-need plants in high-water sprinkler zones and drought-resistant plants in low-water zones. Put your lawn on a separate zone or zones. Then adjust the timing for each zone to match the water needs of that zone. This will allow you to make the best use of your irrigation water whether the supply is plentiful or restricted.

Establishing different water-usage zones will ease the pain of horticultural triage during drought times. You might be able to give your trees and shrubs enough water to survive even as you withhold water from your annuals and lawn. The rule should be: Put your water where your money is. Turf will be the cheapest thing to restart when water availability resumes, and you can always start afresh next spring with annuals. A thousand-dollar tree is more valuable than ten dollars' worth of lawn seed. (See the "Drought-Resistant Plants" list in the Appendix.)

• Electric valves—typically one for each zone. A valve allows water to flow to the output devices on that zone when signaled by the electrical controller.

• Wiring to connect the electric valves with the timer-controller.

• Delivery pipe to get the water from your main water line to the valves and then from the valves out to the areas needing water. Use a 1-inch diameter pipe. It should be buried deep enough to keep it from cracking and freezing in wintertime; in the milder regions west of the Cascades, this could mean 18 inches deep for pipe going from the valves out to the sprinklers. There are many levels of pipe quality in use, but considering the value of your time (or that of whoever digs the trenches and lays the pipe), it only makes sense to buy the best pipe available. If you use the rigid white PVC pipe, Schedule 40 pipe is superb. It will accept 480 pounds of test pressure

before bursting. You can just about drive nails with it. I have even built greenhouse frames and playground climbers out of it. Class 200 is the next best choice in PVC pipe; it will hold 200 pounds of pressure. Avoid the much-thinner-walled Class 125 or less PVC pipe. If you install your own PVC pipe, avoid breathing the fumes of the primer and plastic cement used to seal connections on it. Since PVC turns brittle rather quickly upon contact with ultraviolet radiation from sunlight, it is really only suitable for underground use.

Many irrigation experts prefer the flexible black polyethylene pipe, which also comes in several thicknesses. As mentioned above, this pipe is especially useful if you choose drip irrigation or one of the mini-spray-head systems that connect to the delivery pipe with "spaghetti" tubing. Some polyethylene pipe systems use pressure-fit adaptor bushings with stainless-steel C-clamps instead of chemicals at connecting joints. A few professional irrigation supply houses carry another black plastic pipe material made of polypropylene that uses hybrid connectors made of PVC fittings with preglued barbed adaptor bushings. Both polyethylene and polypropylene have far greater resistance than PVC to ultraviolet radiation from sunlight, so they are suitable for either aboveground or belowground use.

I don't recommend galvanized pipe for sprinkler systems. Beyond its astronomical cost these days, and the great difficulty of installing it, there is the onerous problem of making repairs. I have seen far too many ancient galvanized systems abandoned because of invisible corrosion.

◆ Automatic and manual drains to allow water to drain from the delivery pipes after each use. This is especially important for preparing your system for winter. It gives you an extra measure of protection against freeze damage, even if your pipe is presumably buried deep enough.

◆ A soil-moisture sensor that will shut off the sprinkler system if there is already sufficient water in the soil. It can help prevent superfluous watering. (If you don't have this device, turn your electronic water clock system to standby status on rainy days; you won't end up sprinkling things uselessly during downpours, yet your zone watering settings will be secure for when you need them again.)

◆ Miscellanous supplies, including valve control boxes.

　　Note: It's very important to test each zone of the sprinkler system *before you bury the pipes* so you can make any changes while it's still easy to do.

RULES FOR EFFICIENT WATERING: Once the system is in, your plants will benefit the most, and you'll be using water most efficiently, if you adhere to as many of the following rules as possible.

◆ Soil moisture is more important than the amount of water you dump on your yard. Dense soils that hold water well will need less water than sandy soils that dry out quickly. Try to keep your soil damp, not soaking, 2 inches below the surface of the ground.

◆ Early-morning watering (6:00 to 8:00 A.M.) is better than afternoon or evening watering for most plants. Morning water is more likely to soak down to root levels than water delivered in the heat of the day, when most of it can evaporate. And if you're watering overhead rather than soaking the roots, morning water won't stay on plant leaves for as long as an evening watering. Wet leaves in the cool of the evening encourage disease growth, and evening–water-cooled soil can slow plant growth in the early and late parts of the planting season.

◆ On most soils, deep, infrequent watering is better than frequent, shallow watering. It encourages deep roots and enables plants to survive in times of inadequate water. This means that proper soil preparation, as discussed earlier in this chapter, is vital. Deep watering is impossible for shallow soils situated over impenetrable subsoils, or for extremely sandy soils that retain little water.

◆ When runoff starts, shut off the water. Any water applied after runoff is wasted.

◆ Automatic sprinkler systems with moisture meters can ensure that plants get sufficient water—when and if they need it. Because moisture meters are an emerging technology, I encourage you to pay attention to them occasionally so that you know they are working right.

SYSTEM MAINTENANCE: Although this book concentrates on the design and construction side of landscaping, there are a few steps vital to long-term survival for your irrigation system. The most important step is winter servicing, which you do before the first hard frost of late fall. For aboveground systems, this means disconnecting the anti-siphon device and timing valve, draining them, and keeping them inside over the winter. For underground systems, drain the entire system by shutting off the main controlling valve; run the timer through its paces with the water pressure off; open up manual system drains if you have them. Next spring, close all drains, hook up disconnected items, and run the system again, keeping a close lookout for overly wet spots or other signs of hidden cracks in the pipe.

Mulches

It may seem premature, in a chapter about site preparation, to mention mulches. They normally aren't applied until after all the prep work and plantings have been completed. Besides their obvious uses for weed control, visual beautification, and contribution to soil enrichment, mulches also help to enhance drainage control and irrigation.

The most popular mulch in the Northwest is made from ground-up bark from Douglas fir or Western hemlock. It can last for several years before it eventually rots away into humus; coarser grinds, or chunk bark, will take longer to decompose than finer grinds. If you live in a windy area, consider using the coarser grinds; they're less likely to blow away.

Sometimes people use composted mulches, usually consisting of sawdust that has been mixed with thoroughly processed sludge from sewage treatment plants. As I mentioned above in the section on soil amendments, you should probably restrict use of these mulches to your ornamental gardens.

Some people also use sawdust or wood shavings as a mulch. I like wood shavings as a covering for children's playground areas, because their resilience helps cushion falls, but I am not fond of the appearance of shavings or sawdust as a general mulch, and neither will last as long as bark. You might consider using them in areas away from your front yard, or to cover a very large area economically.

If you prune your own shrubs and trees, you can either buy or rent a power grinder to reduce your trimmings to mulch. These days, the equipment rental fee could be less than the cost of hauling the trimmings to the dump. Again, you should avoid using grindings from Western red cedar except in areas where you don't intend to grow plants for a few years; it will act as a natural weed suppressant.

Any of these mulches will have a similar effect on

Mulches aid in weed control, beautification, soil enrichment, drainage, and irrigation.

erosion control. Forty percent or more of the water that would normally run off downhill gets trapped into the mulch, which directs the water downward into the soil. Only on fairly steep slopes, or on slopes with great quantities of water coming from uphill, will the mulch itself begin to give way and wash downhill. This is a sure sign that you need to change the angle of the slope!

Plants also can help to slow the flow of surface water on your slopes. Although almost any plant roots help to stabilize the soil, groundcover plants help even more because their leaves and branches lie across the soil and act as a physical barrier to slow down the water. Combined with one of the mulches discussed above, a groundcover can be extremely effective in keeping your soil in place. Look at the extended plant listings in the Appendix for suggested groundcovers for our area.

CHAPTER NINE

Construction Techniques

Making Fences, Paths, Patios, Walls, Rockeries, and Ponds

After all the planning is done, it's time to turn the plan into action. In this chapter, we'll cover the fundamentals of several types of landscape construction projects, including fences, paths, patios, retaining walls, and ornamental pools. Along the way, we will discuss how to choose the

**Japanese-style fence with open top section.
(Design by Keith Geller)**

**Open-slat fence controls foot traffic but lets in light and air.
(Scott Lankford design)**

Timber fence and steps.

construction materials that fit your budget and landscaping needs.

Fences

In this section, we will examine the basics of building a fence. Certainly, though, you could also choose to plant a hedge to create a living barrier instead of constructing a fence. Your decision will depend upon your needs, budget, and landscaping style. But if you want a tall, impenetrable barrier immediately, then you'll need either a solid fence or a thickly planted, tall hedge. Building a fence will probably cost considerably less than purchasing mature hedging plants. If you use pressure-treated posts, a fence will probably need less maintenance than a hedge too. And a fence won't need water, fertilizer, or pruning.

There are several reasons you might want to add a fence to your landscape design:

- To keep neighbors, neighbors' pets, or strangers out of your yard—or at least to establish traffic patterns;
- To create a safe play area for your own children, or to keep your pets from straying;
- To screen off an undesirable view;
- To increase security around hazardous elements in your yard such as a sudden drop-off, a pool, or a hot tub.

If, then, a fence is what you need, the next step is to plan what it will look like.

DESIGNING THE FENCE: Different needs translate into different fence designs. If you need a private area in your yard, or if you need to completely screen off an unattractive sight, you'll want to build a solid fence that nobody can see through. If you are trying to redirect or prevent foot (or paw) traffic but you don't want to block light or wind, then a more open fence pattern can work out well.

The typical Northwest fence is made of wood: posts concreted into the ground, rails strung between the posts, and boards nailed to the rails. But within these constraints there is room for variation in design.

You can design a solid fence with either a vertical or a horizontal pattern. Vertical is the more common design and is easier to build, but you can also make a horizontal pattern to match the clapboard siding typically used on Northwest houses. The most popular sizes used in solid fencing are 1"x6" and 1"x4" boards. I like 1"x2" or 2"x2" boards, especially for small fences, because they can add a touch of delicacy that is missing from the larger-slab fences. The appearance of the wood is important too. Most lumberyards carry both smooth-sided and rough-sided fencing boards. Some sawmills produce a very rough fence stake that looks fine in a rustic setting. Your budget and landscape style may dictate whether you use wood that is clear-grade (no knotholes and very expensive), tight-knot, or loose-knot. Choose the finish that best matches your landscape style and use it consistently.

A driftwood fence, perfect for a casual coastal landscape.

Ornamental iron fence. (Design adapted by Mike Kowalski)

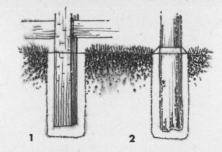

1. Treated wood post, anchored in concrete. Rails are toenailed into the post. 2. For untreated wood, shape a collar of concrete to deflect water away from the wood.

Some fences combine a solid pattern on the bottom with a latticework or open-slat top. This can be a good compromise between screening out snoops and letting in light, although stapled, prefabricated lattices have become a visual cliché.

Open-slat fences serve as excellent traffic stoppers while letting in a maximum amount of light and air. They work well when you have notable scenery beyond the fence, allowing you to pull those sights into your garden space. They also can be reassuring if you live in a security-conscious neighborhood because you can always tell as you approach your gate what lies beyond.

♦

Choose the type of board finish that best matches your landscape style, and use it consistently.

♦

One rustic fence favorite is old-fashioned split cedar. It's not meant as a security fence, but it will redirect most foot traffic. I usually think of it as most suitable for a casual suburban or rural site, but I have also seen it used effectively in an English-style cottage garden in the city.

In Pacific Northwest beachfront gardens, I often see attractive fences made out of pieces of scavenged driftwood, stood side by side on end and secured to the ground with concrete. Their bleached-gray color and natural forms blend perfectly with the sandy or cobbly beach and with the frequent clouds on the horizon.

Because neither split cedar nor driftwood is pressure-treated, any part that comes into contact with the ground will be subject to attack by insects and microorganisms. You can make these kinds of fences last longer by soaking the bottom of the posts with a suitable wood preservative or sealant. Another trick is to slope the concrete footing as you set the wood-ends into place, to encourage water to drain away from the posts where they contact the soil. This will delay the day when you will have to redo the posts.

What are some alternatives to a wood fence? Ornamental welded iron is probably the most elegant of all fencing material. It is especially well suited to very formal or highly structured environments, such as upscale city neighborhoods or brickwork-laden suburban estates. You're not limited to the standard vertical-bar-with-spike-top. Because iron is so malleable when it's hot, you can create many fanciful or playful designs with it: fleurs-de-lis, the family crest, Chinese dragons, cornucopias, asymmetrical abstracts. If you don't have welding equipment in the garage, you'll have to hire someone to do the actual work, and it will cost lots of money; but if the budget allows and it fits your landscape style, you can create something really special. I know of one family who, when they moved, wrote into their real-estate contract that their iron front gates went with them. I am not impressed with the mass-market stamped-metal, imitation–cast-iron fencework I have seen; it may look good initially and have an attractive price, but it doesn't hold up the way real iron fencework will.

Chain link is not my favorite fencing material. It is not friendly and cannot be made to look friendly, even if you stuff wood or plastic lathing down through its slots or buy it clad with colored vinyl. It is useful where you need a relatively cheap, long-lasting material to cover a lot of territory. If you decide to go with it, consider softening its appearance by covering it with espaliered fruit trees, climbing roses, or vines. A chain-link fence can support even rampant vines such as kiwi (*Actinidia* spp.) or wisteria, which would be far too aggressive for a lightweight trellis or lattice. Unless you have experience with a chain-link fence puller and other specialized tools, compare the cost of doing it yourself with estimates from some contractors before you begin.

A less expensive and more attractive alternative to chain link is welded wire. It can be mounted onto special metal stakes that you pound into the ground with a sledgehammer. Such a fence works well in a rural site as a casual, utilitarian enclosure around a vegetable garden or chicken run. But you can also spend a little more money and mount the welded wire onto a wooden post-and-rail frame to give it a more finished appearance. I have seen this kind of fencing used effectively even in very exclusive neighborhoods. If the wooden framework is substantial enough, you can use it like chain link to support just about any sort of vine. Look for heavy-gauge, galvanized welded wire at feed stores or complete hardware/lumber stores. It will serve you far better than the lightweight vinyl-coated wire fencing that is sometimes sold as a consumer item. If you have even moderate construction skills, you should be able to make a decent-looking welded-wire fence. A fence puller could be helpful here too, but welded wire is far easier to maneuver than chain link.

ESTIMATING WOOD FENCE MATERIALS: Begin by determining the amount of lumber and other materials you will need. Take into account that smooth-finish wood will be smaller than rough wood of the same nominal dimensions; although a rough 1"x4" might be close to those dimensions, the same board after planing and smoothing will be closer to ⅝"x3½". For a "solid" wood fence, you will want to have at least a ¼-inch gap between boards to allow for milling irregularities and for expansion and contraction of the wood as it reacts to heat, cold, moisture, and dryness. As an example, a fence 100 feet long made of finished 1"x4" boards would need 320 boards — (100' x 12") ÷ (3.5" + 0.25").

Most fences will need 4"x4" pressure-treated posts placed every 8 feet (either center to center or inside edge to inside edge) for support. If you go longer than 8 feet, you increase the chances that your fence will start to sag between posts as gravity drags the rails down. Your fence will look as if someone had let the air out of its tires. Most gates should be no more than 4 feet wide, or they'll sag too.

You'll need a 60-pound bag of concrete mix to anchor each post into the ground. Our 100-foot fence would need about 13 posts (110 ÷ 8) and 13 bags of concrete. You'll need more if you put in any gates. Add 2 feet to the height of the fence you want to build to determine what length posts you will need; a 4-foot-high fence will need 6-foot-long posts, with the additional 2 feet buried in the ground. You can also use concrete mix to anchor H-shaped iron strapping brackets to the ground, and mount posts of the proper height to the brackets. Either method will make a secure framework for the fence. I like to use the brackets for those sections of fence that might have to be removed occasionally to let large equipment pass through; you can just unbolt the posts from the brackets and swing the sections aside.

Chances are good that you will use 2"x4" boards for your rails. I prefer to use pressure-treated wood for the rails, but that is not as critical as using pressure-treated posts. Use fence clips or rail brackets (two for each rail) if you want to make it easy to remove sections of fence later. Otherwise, you can just toenail the rails to the posts. Our simple 100-foot fence would need twenty-six 2"x4" rail boards and fifty-two small fence brackets.

If your fence will need to hold extra weight, consider using thicker posts (4"x6" or 6"x6") and sturdier rails (2"x6"). This holds true especially if you plan to cover the fence frame with clapboard siding, shakes, or other heavy wood.

There is a wide range of quality in nails; I hope you can find some strong ones. Galvanized nails work well in most wood, although they may discolor Western red cedar a bit.

Beyond a healthy supply of wood and nails, you will also need one or two 4-foot-long bubble levels, a line bubble level, and enough strong line cord to stretch from one corner of the fence to the other. This is in addition to the more obvious tools: claw hammer, electric circular saw, carpenter's pencil, measuring tape, safety goggles, wheelbarrow and shovel for mixing concrete, a supply of clean water, and a posthole digger. (If your soil has any rocks at all, get a rock bar to help you with the holes, or you'll destroy the posthole digger.) And don't forget the hinges and gate latch.

You will need to protect the wood after it is installed. This means, at least, a transparent stain or sealant to minimize damage from weathering. Or it could mean a semitransparent colored stain or even a solid paint.

BUILDING A WOOD FENCE: Place the corner posts first, using the 4-foot level to make sure the posts are as vertical as possible. Using your wheelbarrow, mix one bag of concrete with just enough water to make a thick slurry and pour it around the first corner post. Repeat until you have placed all of the corner posts. Let them set well; this can take a day or so. While you wait for that, you can begin to dig the other holes. You probably will want the holes to be in a straight line, unless you are building a meandering fence among existing trees. String up your line between the corner posts and begin to spot where the connecting posts will go. You can mark the places with stakes, take down the string for now, and start digging your holes. They should be about 2 feet deep. Don't use the posthole digger to hammer holes into the ground. If the ground is hard-packed or rocky, use your rock bar to knock material loose, and then use the posthole digger to pull out what you've loosened.

Once all the remaining holes are dug and the corner posts have hardened in their spots, string the line up again and make it taut between the corner posts. Install the remaining posts, using the level to make sure the posts are perfectly vertical in all directions, and pour in a bag of prepared, mixed concrete mix for each post. When the concrete dries in a day or so, you can begin to put up your rails. In most cases, you will want to use a level to make sure the rails are horizontal; then stretch a string across the top of the posts as a guide for attaching the fence boards. I like to use a small spacer between the fence boards so that I'm sure there will be a consistent gap.

Gates are easier to build if they're flat on the ground rather than standing in the air. If you are good at measuring, get the lengths of the top and bottom gate rails by measuring the gap between gateposts. I prefer to leave about a ¼- to ½-inch gap top and bottom between the gate and gateposts to allow room for the hinges and eventual post settling or leaning. After you make the gate frame, you can help its long-term stability with a diagonal brace. Place the lower end of the diagonal pointing toward the lower gate hinge, and the upper end aimed at the gate latch. You'll probably need a helper to get the gate installed onto the fence—to hold it upright while you drill hinge holes and attach the hinge screws.

Even if you use pressure-treated wood for the entire fence, you may want to cover it either to decorate or protect it. A wood sealant can help prevent water damage by sealing water out. A stain can help do the same, while adding a degree of color. Although you may have to redo the sealant or stain after some years, it's not very complicated to do so. Paint is effective if you want to match the fence to the color of your house; but you might end up with increased maintenance because of eventual chipping or bubbling of the paint. Proper repair to the painted surface could include stripping off the existing paint before repainting. This is really tedious, and you could find yourself resenting all the work. I don't recommend lacquer for fences for the same reason. No matter which of these products you use, make sure the fence wood is dry before you apply any coating. Unlike household lumber, fence lumber

♦

A wood sealant or stain can help protect your fence by sealing water out.

♦

Interlocking pavers in an informal design. (Jerry Munro)

is not likely to be kiln dried. If you cover it too soon, you could end up sealing moisture in, which would create more problems later, especially premature wood rot and blistering paint.

Paths and Patios

I've decided to talk about paths and patios together because they are made from the same range of materials and have complementary purposes.

Although we usually use paths when we want to move and patios when we want to rest, there's not really a clear dividing line. Oftentimes one flows visually into the other.

♦ Use wide, direct paths in straight lines or gentle curves as major thoroughfares where people or garden supplies must move freely. In all but the smallest gardens, 3 feet is a good minimum width for these paths.

♦ Try narrow, winding paths to encourage close-up inspections of planting beds. Irregular steps, perhaps only a foot across, could be big enough.

♦ A patio near the house and the major pathways signals a general meeting area. Certainly, the larger the patio is, the larger the meeting or yard party can be.

♦ A patio or cranny at the end of an obscure path celebrates privacy. The smaller it is, the more private it can be.

CHOOSING THE MATERIAL: The type of material you use for paths and patios will have a profound influence on the overall effect you achieve in your garden, from rustic to classic. The secret of success lies in choosing just a few materials and using them consistently to bring visual harmony to your landscape plan.

♦ Loose materials, such as crushed gravel, shavings, or wood chips, are perfect for naturalistic gardens. Pea gravel is great to view, but for real-life use by humans, it is a Keystone Kops paving material.

Avoid it unless you enjoy the sensation of walking on ball bearings and don't need to move wheelbarrows or garden equipment through it. And avoid colored gravel if you have any overhanging trees in the yard, because tree debris will contaminate the gravel quickly.

- You can take those same loose materials and make them more formal by using one of several edgings: 2"x4" boards, bender board, plastic or metal edging, or brick. All of these work well to keep loose paving material from mingling with the soil or bark mulch outside the path. Edgings are described in greater detail in Chapter 11, "Lawns."

- Dry-laid (without mortar) brick, flat rock, and interlocking pavers can all add an element of structure to a yard. They often benefit from having edging to help hold them in place, but that is not an absolute requirement. They will flex with minor soil movement, thus they retain their good looks. I like the interlocking concrete pavers because they give a bricklike appearance, they don't get as slippery when wet as some brick does, and they are very strong. They are machined so closely that do-it-yourselfers can fit them together easily. There are now several different colors and patterns on the market. Regular brick is harder for do-it-yourselfers to work, but you can do well if you take extra care.

- Recycled chunks of broken concrete make good pavers. Landscape architect Keith Geller tore out a decrepit concrete walkway in his yard, flipped the chunks over, rotated some of them so they would not be an inverse image of the old walkway, added a few cobbles as accents, and mortared everything in place. The rough new surface fits nicely with the rustic elements in his yard. (See Chapter 7, "Visions of the Garden," for a description of Geller's garden.)

- Poured concrete is the chameleon of paving surfaces. It can have casual curves or formal straight lines; its surface can be smooth, brushed, colored, or texturized, or can include smooth or crushed aggregates in a wide range of colors. Concrete is also the most treacherous paving material to install. I do not recommend extensive, wet concrete work for do-it-yourselfers, unless you've had a chance to practice in some other victim's yard. Because of its rigidity after drying, concrete will often show cracks as time passes and the soil underneath subsides or nearby trees flex their roots.

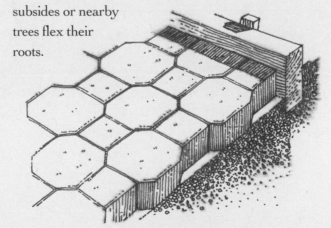

Pavers with a straight edging. Compacted sand is used underneath; more sand is brushed over the pavers afterward.

◆ Wooden decks and walkways can be considered types of patios and paths too. The main difference between wood and other materials is that wood is usually suspended above the ground. Landscape architect Bud Merrill notes that decks can be especially useful in areas where tree roots are a problem. Other than the posts and post blocks, no other part of a deck touches the ground, so tree roots are not likely to disturb the level of the deck. Gaps in the wood should let through a considerable amount of rainfall to nourish tree and shrub roots.

LAYING THE FOUNDATION: For any type of path or patio, you will need to carve the underlying soil as closely as possible to its final grade and then pack it down with a water-filled roller. If you're thinking of using concrete, get a heavy-duty roller or power vibrator to tamp the soil down. Grade patios so they drain away from the house or toward a convenient catch basin.

If you want to lay loose material such as crushed gravel or shavings over muddy soil, begin with some DuPont Mirafi™ fabric. This will keep the mud from mixing in with the paving material and making a grand mess, yet will allow the natural flow of air and water through the soil. I have seen this fabric used with good results on heavily traveled park trails in our coastal rain forest. If you can't locate any Mirafi, note that some of the thicker-fabric weed barriers can also act as mud barriers. On

drier soils, you might still consider using a weed barrier beneath loose paving materials to cut down on maintenance.

Brick and interlocking pavers, with their symmetrical shapes, can add a touch of European formality to gardens. Dry-laid brick, flat stone, and interlocking pavers benefit greatly and are much easier to install if you use at least 2 inches of sand underneath. Crushed gravel with fines (unsifted crushed gravel that still contains the grit and sand) also works well as an underlayment. Compact the underlayer well. If you are working with thin, flat stones, you might want to dig a hole where each stone is to go and fill it with a wet concrete or mortar mix. Then settle the stone into the mix and let it set.

For mortared brick and rock, start by putting down a 2- to 3-inch-thick concrete underlayment slab, letting it set, and then surfacing it with the brick or rock, using mortar to keep it all in place. If you want to replace an existing patio or walkway, you have two choices: Rip out the existing material, or use it as a sturdy underlayment and mortar the new material on top. If you use real brick, make sure it is paving brick, which has a tough surface that resists buildup of moss and wintertime cracking and flaking.

Retaining Walls

Rock and wood are the most common materials used in Northwest walls. They are inexpensive, abundant, and can look rather attractive when properly used. Modular building blocks are a good alternative if you want something solid like rock but easier to fit together. Any of these is a good prospect for the do-it-yourselfer with a strong back, a deep respect for heavy objects, and a few simple tools.

How high can you build? You'll need a permit to build anything above 30 inches high. This might be a good maximum height for a do-it-yourself wall, unless you have an overriding need to build higher than that—a particularly steep site, for instance.

RAILROAD TIES AND TIMBERS: Wood that touches the ground will not last long without protection. Moisture, insects, and microorganisms are among the many forces working against it. If you want a permanent wood wall, you must use pressure-treated wood.

Railroad ties have been the traditional favorite for Northwest yards. They are relatively easy to work with, they come in fairly standard sizes, they are cheap, they are pressure-treated, they are sufficiently bulky to be built into substantial walls, and they can be cut to interesting shapes and fastened together with special long nails.

They are also more practical than attractive, especially when used in intimate-scale or classic landscapes. Fresh railroad ties with a strong scent and a sticky black coating are likely to leach creosote into the surrounding soil and onto shoes and clothes. This

Ties and timbers allow great design flexibility. Twelve-inch spikes join succeeding layers. In this retaining wall, terraced boxes increase stability and add interest.

THERE ARE IMPORTANT structural issues to keep in mind if you are building tie or timber retaining walls.

◆ Avoid long, straight walls if you can. A wood wall more than 24 feet long can be visually imposing, but the visual effect might be gained at the expense of stability. Overlapping boxes or changes in line will increase the structural stability and decrease the possibility (and noticeability) of wall movement caused by pressure from the fill soil on the uphill side.

◆ For a tall wall (over 30 inches high), purchase only sound wood, with no major signs of splitting or disintegration. This is particularly important with ties, which can be many decades old before they arrive in your yard and sometimes have been subjected to considerable abuse. Go to the seller and examine the ties before you buy them. Picking them out one by one is tedious, but that way you know what you're getting; some "bundled" groups of ties have all the bad ties hidden in the center.

◆ Use a long, accurate bubble level or string-line level to make sure the wall starts level and stays level as you add each layer. A 4-foot-long level attached to a straight 8-foot two-by-four can help you avoid being fooled by minor variations in the surface of the ties. Crushed gravel makes a good shimming material for ties.

◆ Put the base row of ties or timbers on solid ground. If you're not sure you're on solid ground, start digging until you're sure.

◆ Overlap each layer of ties as you stack them. Nail each layer into the layer below with 12"x½" steel nails—at least two per tie. You'll need a sledgehammer to pound the nails in. Wear goggles while you're pounding.

◆ Use deadmen to help stabilize the wall against the hill. These are ties placed perpendicular to the wall, pointing straight back into the hill, which are attached to the wall with the same long steel nails and then covered with fill soil. They are typically 4 feet long—a full tie or timber cut in half. Bury the deadmen as you build up the wall; the only thing that should reveal their presence is the butt end, visible where it is attached to the front side of the wall. Behind the wall, fill soil and plantings will hide these wooden anchors.

◆ A slight tilt (perhaps 5 degrees) back into the hill can also help to minimize pressure on the top side of the wall.

limits their usefulness in raised vegetable beds and makes them unsuitable for walking or sitting on. Ties are most useful in informal landscapes, where their massiveness can be softened with concealing ground-covers, or in very large yards, where their size in comparison with the surrounding territory will not be overwhelming. Certainly it is far easier for a do-it-yourselfer to make a decent-looking railroad tie wall than to make a satisfactory masonry wall.

A more modern alternative to railroad ties is pressure-treated timber. For small-scale walls (under 2 feet high), 4"x6" lumber, available at most lumber-yards, might be sufficient. But for larger-scale walls, you should seek out suppliers who have 6"x8" or larger timbers. Avoid using "cherry-tone" wood which has not been pressure-treated. You will see it advertised very cheaply as "landscape timbers," but it is *not* suitable for permanent ground contact.

Pressure-treated timbers have some distinct advantages over railroad ties:

- They are often neat enough to merit use in tidier gardens.
- They can be stained or painted to match or complement the color of other wood structures nearby.
- The chemicals used will probably be much less haz-ardous to your soil than creosote—but check with the vendor.
- The wood will be much easier to cut because there will be no ground-in dirt and gravel, as there so

often is on used ties. (Smart equipment-rental shopowners forbid the use of their chain saws on railroad ties.)

ROCK WALLS AND OTHER STRUCTURES: Rocks make perfect sense in many Northwest yards. They come with the territory. In areas scoured by glaciers or rivers, they are smooth and rounded; in places with lots of seismic activity, they are broken-edged and fractured. Sometimes you can see the two types close together: a stream or river flows through a sharp cut of mountain, giving us smooth, water-worn rocks below flanked by rising walls of rough basalt. Is it any wonder, with so much of it around, that we find uses for rock in our yards? Rocks may seem neither practical nor ornamental if you've been removing endless numbers of them from the site of your future lawn area. In the right place, though, rocks have many uses in Northwest landscaping—in retaining walls, shotgun rockeries, and as outcrop-pings, discussed below; in real or artificial water-ways; and as pathways or stepping stones.

Because so much of our housing is built into the sides of hills, we often use rock to help hold the hill-sides together. Sometimes such a wall of rock will be built in a straight line, with a level top and a nearly vertical face. But you might also see rock walls that wrap around hillsides, following the broad contours of the land. You may also see rockeries with pockets of soil to allow the planting of trees or shrubs. This

A small rockery retaining wall. The right side is better than the left: Try not to stack all rocks directly on top of each other.

A simple outcropping on a hillside: two companion rocks grouped together.

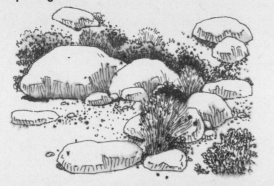

An alternative to a shotgun rockery: Vary rock size and placement to give a pleasing natural arrangement.

suppleness of line can help to soften the inherent sternness of most rock used in rock walls.

In the Northwest, we don't usually mortar individual rocks together. You will see some mortared rock walls around, either in older urban areas or where the owner is looking for a particular effect. Rounder rocks work well in mortared walls. Most Northwest rock walls are not free-standing. Instead, the rocks rely upon their sheer bulk, gravity, careful placement in relation to each other, and proper back-filling to keep them in place.

Placing the Rock: If you are good with jigsaw puzzles, then you might also be good at do-it-yourself rock walls. The spatial-relations skills are very similar, although making a rockery involves far more physical work. The placement of individual rocks becomes especially important because rocks do not come in standardized shapes. Each has its own personality. Some will be wedge-shaped, some will be almost flat, some will be blocky, some will be rounded or indented on certain corners. Each rock must be examined and judged, not just for where it should fit into the wall, but for what direction it should face. Which side makes the best base for the rock? With a wedge-shaped or flat rock, you have the choice of either standing it vertically so that it shows the most face, or laying it flat. This might tempt you to stand a number of rocks on edge to make a cheaper wall. But horizontal placement is much more stable. Consider two people, side by side, one standing and the other sitting. Push both of them, and see who moves more easily. In the same fashion, the soil behind the wall will constantly push against it, challenging your placement of the rocks and seeking to push through any weak spots.

It's not just flat and wedge-shaped rocks that make potentially unstable spots in a rockery. Anytime you try to stack up rocks that don't have a reasonably flat bottom and top, you decrease the stability of the wall. Sometimes you can place two poorly shaped rocks together to make a firmer footing for the next-higher rock, but occasionally you will find rocks that defeat your attempts to fit them into the wall. Don't be reluctant to use them for fill behind the wall or to use them elsewhere in the yard as outcroppings.

To increase the stability of the rockery, put the biggest rocks at the bottom of the wall and work your way up to the smallest at the top. This will make it easier for you, since you won't have to lift the big rocks as high. Be sure to examine the soil where you want to place the rockery. If the soil is soft and easy to dig into, either because it's too sandy or because it's too muddy, you are not yet ready to start installing rock. You must dig down to solid ground, and place the footing rocks on bearing soil. If you are at all unsure what to look for, call in some expert help. This could be a soils engineer, a rockery contractor, or both.

As with the building of any major structure, make sure you do your homework before you begin. If you are going to work near your property lines, ask your local building and land use department about minimum allowable setbacks (how close to the street or property lines you can build), maximum heights, and required or recommended backfill for your wall.

Materials and Equipment: Before you start, you should determine how much material you will need, and what kind: the rock itself, the fill dirt or topsoil to build up the soil level behind the wall, and spalls (crushed rock) to keep the fill material from sifting through the rocks.

How much rock will you need? If you have put together a topographical map, you will have a better idea. One ton of one-man rock will cover about 18 to 20 square feet of rockery face. Ten tons could make a rockery about 3 feet high and 60 feet or so in length, or about 180 square feet. If you use two- or three-man rock, the same 10 tons of rock would cover only about 120 to 150 square feet. As mentioned above, how you place the rock can make a substantial difference in how much area it will cover. Some of this coverage—the part used as footing—will be hidden by soil after you are finished.

Cross-section of rock wall. Note two possible slopes behind the wall: rising for wet areas, falling for dry.

The size of the rock you use will vary with the height of the wall; the higher the wall, the larger the rocks should be. For low walls, up to 2 feet or so high, you could use small rock. By this, I do not mean rubble-sized. At a minimum, the rocks should be what are called "one-man rocks," which weigh from about 80 to 250 pounds. This does not mean one man or woman can lift them; it means one person can budge a one-man rock with a strong steel prybar.

If you hope to install a rockery without power equipment, one-man rock is about as big as you will want to use. Even if you do decide to use small rock, you might still want to have some power equipment handy. A backhoe or a small tractor could be helpful in digging out a footing of solid ground for the rockery, for moving and lifting the rock into place, and for backfilling with the proper support material. If you need to build a wall higher than 2 feet, you should use bigger rock, and you will definitely need a large machine for moving the rock. This means a cherry picker with a hydraulic clamshell, and preferably a skilled human operator.

I do not recommend using one-man rock if you intend to place some other kind of substantial structure, such as a tall fence, concrete patio, carport, or driveway, above the rockery. Use larger rocks, or consider installing a poured concrete wall instead.

For large rockeries, you might find it most convenient to have the rock delivered from one of the local quarries, since rock is always cheaper at the source. If you have a choice of several quarries and some time to spare, drive out to the quarries to see what kind of rock they are currently extracting. There might be some differences in color or quality that will influence your choice. For example, you don't want "pudding" rock, which will crumble after exposure to a few winters. Once you find your preferred rock source, order all your rock from that one source; your rockery will blend together better if you do.

For a smaller rockery, if you have a sturdy pickup truck and are willing to load rocks onto the truck yourself, you might be able to hand-pick and load the most suitable rocks, as opposed to having a quarry deliver them. This is usually more feasible when you are choosing flat rocks for walkways and stairways, since they will be relatively smaller and easier to handle. (Another good reason for choosing and loading the rocks yourself is that you will have absolute control over the shapes and sizes of the rocks you get. Although you might have the privilege of refusing delivery of a load of rocks if you think some are too large for your purposes, sometimes a truckload of rock can hold unpleasant surprises that are not apparent until after the load has been dumped. At that point, it's your problem alone.)

Other good—although expensive—places to find flat rock are specialty rock yards, building materials yards, or stone supply houses. These places deal with rocks suitable for building siding, fireplaces, and free-standing mortared rock walls. Again, you usually have a choice between home delivery or pickup. I have also built many "rock" walls using broken-chunk concrete. If you have access to a construction site where concrete is being removed, it can make an attractive wall, especially if all the pieces are of the same thickness. And the concrete might be free for the taking, if you supply the labor and transportation.

Quarries are also the perfect place to find suitable backfill material for the wall: crushed rock, or spalls. For every three or four tons of rock, you should expect to use about a ton of backfill. The crushed rock should be large enough to stay in place, not drift out through the crevices between rocks. By getting the backfill from the same source as your rock, you are more likely to get a match of color, so that any backfill that does show will blend in with the face rock.

Outcroppings: In nature, an outcropping is a section of rock, perhaps on a hillside or near water, that is partially revealed and partially concealed by the surrounding soil. It might consist of a small number of rocks, two or three or so, aligned together. All of them will typically be facing in the same outward direction, and all of the tops will be flat or nearly so. If it is a sedimentary rock outcropping, with definite lines visible within it, these strata will be aligned in the same sedimental direction. Any outcropping you

WORKING SAFELY WITH ROCK

ROCKERIES PRESENT one of the easier ways for do-it-yourselfers to injure themselves. Typically, people try to lift or move by hand rocks bigger than they can manage, or they have their fingers in the wrong place when shifting rocks by hand. You can minimize the risk by making clever use of some simple tools and rules.

◆ Use a large prybar for moving large rocks, and smaller prybars for making minor adjustments in spacing. Shovels are strictly for shoveling loose dirt, not prying rocks.

◆ Don't carry rock directly in your hands. Rocks are awkward because they weigh so much compared to their size. Make a hammock or sling out of strong burlap or canvas. Roll the rock onto it and have two or more people carry the sling rather than the rock. This lowers your load's center of gravity and makes the rock much more manageable—and if the rock should slip, it is more likely to hit the ground than someone's hand, leg, or foot.

◆ Know your strength, and work within your limits. Take frequent breaks.

create in your garden, then, will look more natural if you strive for these characteristics.

In a designed landscape, an outcropping can be used to help minimize soil erosion or movement on a hillside where a full-scale rockery would be unnecessary or too intrusive. Outcroppings are also effective when used in berms because they can make the mound of soil look more like an integral part of the landscape, rather than glued on as an afterthought. Too, a berm with outcroppings can be an effective traffic barrier for a house situated on a dangerous corner or at the bottom of a steep hill.

Outcroppings can be the perfect use for rocks with interesting faces whose awkward shapes make them unsuitable for a wall.

An outcropping can also work well as the basis for an alpine or rock garden when the rocks become companions to or backdrops for groups of plants from mountainous regions. If you are a rock-garden fan looking for maximum verisimilitude, ordinary quarry rock might not be satisfactory. You might want to determine what type of rock is native to the mountain region you are trying to simulate and then start searching for specialty rock sources. Expect to pay a premium for any rock that is brought in from far away.

Outcroppings also serve well as visual support for real or artificial streams and ponds. Because a large portion of outcropping rock can (and often should) be hidden beneath the surrounding soil, an outcropping is often a perfect use for rocks with interesting faces whose awkward shapes make them unsuitable for placement in a wall. In Japanese landscapes, you will often see outcroppings of rock, but they are more likely to be primarily exposed, giving the appearance that water has washed away most of the soil that covered them.

Shotgun Rockeries: Shotgun rockeries are the easiest to do, but could be the hardest to do well. They are done on both hillsides and flat ground. Where a rock wall looks highly organized, and an outcropping looks very natural, the shotgun rockery can have an overall random appearance, as if the rocks were individual dots on the landscape. The rocks typically don't touch each other; they are separated by plantings or patches of bare earth. The advantage of this kind of rockery is its ease of construction; much less rock-wrangling is required to fit the rocks together. If you prefer the shotgun style of rockery and are using rough quarry rock, with all its edges and angles, you can increase your chances of success by paying close attention to the orientation of each rock so that, in the end, they all appear to face in a common direction. Rounded field stones will be easier to place aesthetically.

ALTERNATIVE WALL MATERIALS: There are a few other bulkhead materials that may be suitable for do-it-yourself landscapers. I am being cautious here because there are great opportunities to do mischief on a grand, public scale.

Concrete walls are a potential nightmare for the unwary do-it-yourselfer. Unlike brick walls, which go up a brick at a time and where each piece can be installed with care and deliberation, concrete walls are usually poured in a rush. This means that extra-special care must be taken while setting up the wooden forms for the pour. The resulting wall, if done well, can add a touch of elegance to your yard, particularly if the concrete has a textured, patterned, or exposed-aggregate finish. On the other hand, plain concrete can look pedestrian or austere, even unfriendly.

If you do decide to do it yourself, try to get some hands-on experience before you go public. There are sometimes community workshops or vocational-technical classes devoted to training in these skills. Attend them if they are available.

If you like the look of concrete, but don't want to pour concrete, inquire at your building supply center about modular building-block systems which can be fitted together into a solid wall without mortar. Modular block systems are usually concrete blocks shaped and colored to add visual distinction. Modular block walls are more suitable for do-it-yourselfers than poured concrete, yet they can give a landscape project a similar aura of elegance. Because these concrete blocks are manufactured to a standard size, they are easier to fit together than rocks. You don't have to guess about fit, or assemble your wall like a jigsaw puzzle, as you do when building a rock wall. Follow the manufacturer's directions, start from solid ground, use a level as described above in the paragraphs for tie walls, stretch a line across the face of the wall to keep each level perfect, and good luck. Don't be tempted to hurry your pace. May your course be straight and true.

Building an Ornamental Pool

Can you imagine Butchart Gardens without the ponds and fountains? Crater Lake without the lake? Snoqualmie Falls without the falls? Although most of us cannot compete for scale with settings of that splendor in our yards, we realize how much water can contribute to a setting. We love to hear the sound of water trickling down rocks or splashing into pools, and we will travel or hike out of our way to see it when we go touring around the Northwest—although usually we don't have to travel very far. Is it any wonder, then, that we so often try to incorporate water into our landscapes?

In Chapter 3, "Taking Stock," I addressed the issue of safety with water. You will have to take safety into consideration if you want exposed water in your own yard.

A SIMPLE POOL: Proper placement of the pool is important. At the base of outcropping rocks or a

HINTS ON WORKING WITH WATER

THERE ARE SOME WAYS to minimize the initial outlay and eventual maintenance costs associated with an ornamental pool.

◆ Keep the size of your pool small and simple. Even a tiny pool can provide a welcome spot of wetness in the yard. Multiple-level pools with waterfalls cascading from one pool to the next will add beauty and interest, but the more complex design will add expense.

◆ Be on the lookout for creative pool materials. If you're interested in a formal pool, you can check local pool supply yards; or you can shop for livestock water troughs or surplus boiler tank ends. Plunged into the ground and painted a dark color, these improvised pools can hold up for years, and can be remarkably affordable.

◆ Butyl rubber or polyvinyl liners, 30-mil thickness or greater, make very adaptable underpinnings for pools with irregular, naturalistic outlines. Use liners that are approved for use with fish or drinking water to make the basis of your pool. Certain prefabricated ponds and pools might be worth considering—as well as some that look exceedingly artificial. Avoid those with aquamarine reflective bottoms; they look out of place in most Northwest landscapes, and will begin to show dirt and other contamination sooner than you might like. Black or brown pools or liners are unobtrusive.

◆ Avoid unlined concrete. Concrete, either plain or with exposed aggregate, can make a fine-looking pool. But it can crack when subjected to repeated freeze and thaw cycles or to the uneven settling of the surrounding soil. If you use concrete, line the bottom with one of the new pool liners before you pour the concrete. Even if the concrete cracks, the liner should keep the structure watertight.

retaining wall would be a logical choice. I realize that it's tempting to install a pool in a place of prominence in the yard—even next to the driveway or the front entryway. But consider situating yours in a subtle, almost secret place in the back yard (see the Buckles garden in Chapter 7, "Visions of the Garden"). This way, if you have a small fountain or aerator running, people will hear the water before they see it.

Your pool should look as if it belonged in the landscape, not as if it had been tacked on to it. If you have a rockery in the landscape, use the same kind of rock near or within your pool. If most of your rock nearby is of basaltic origin (charcoal gray with occasional contrasting veins), don't decorate the surroundings of the pool with granite (primarily off-white with dark flecks). This is one reason why I usually hesitate to recommend artificial rock specifically designed for a pool—although a prefabricated unit will simplify your construction chores if you are contemplating a waterfall.

Shape the ground in your yard to allow room for an asymmetrical hollow in the soil. Line the soil with enough pool liner to cover the bottom and fit well up and over the sides. You should get a big enough piece of liner to cover everything without any seams. Bury the edges with soil and rocks. Cobblestones or small, rounded fieldstones that match the color of your other rocks will work well. You can then further disguise the liner with plants. Iris is an obvious choice, but *Primula, Astilbe,* and *Leucothoe* also adapt

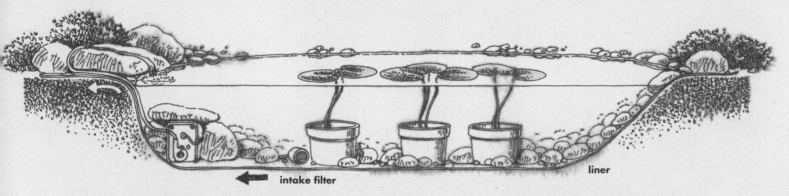

intake filter   liner

Butyl rubber or polyvinyl liner makes a flexible bottom for this simple pond. Rocks on the shore help to anchor the edges of the liner and add a touch of naturalism. The submersible pump (which must be properly grounded to a GFCI circuit) circulates water through a plastic tube to a low-key waterfall that helps to aerate the water.

well to a poolside environment. Plants within the water, such as water lilies, can be plunged container-and-all into the pool. Or you can layer a foot of soil onto the bottom, install your water plants carefully into the soil, and cover the soil with wire-mesh hardware cloth and cobbles to keep down water turbulence.

If you would like to hear the sound of water bubbling in your pool but don't live on a stream, you will need an electric water pump and fountain fixture or outlet tubing. A circulating pump serves as more than mere decoration; it will also oxygenate the water in the pool, which will keep any fish and water plants happy and prevent the swampy smell of stagnant

water, especially if you've put soil onto the bottom of the pool. There are small, submersible pumps that perform this service well. You will need a filter on one end and a tube attached to a fountain or waterfall on the other—and a source of safe 120-volt power. The pump should be plugged into a line with a ground fault circuit interrupter. Place the filter so that it won't be in direct contact with soil.

If you have raccoons in your neighborhood, install a screen of welded wire just below water level to minimize fish and plant loss—or use cheap fish and water plants and expect to replace them regularly. The screen can also serve as a protective device for adventurous young children.

CHAPTER TEN

Planting and Transplanting

Safe and Successful Techniques

*I*n Chapter 1, "Chasing a Vision" we talked about sources for plant material. Plants could come from local nurseries, mail-order firms, or even your own yard. If you have existing plants situated in the wrong place, they might be worth transplanting. Most of the information about planting applies to transplanting as well.

Planting

In the Pacific Northwest, you can buy a plant from a wide range of nursery stock almost any month of the year, dig a hole in the ground, put in the plant, water it erratically, and expect it to survive. Mind you, it may not thrive, but it probably won't die, either. If you really want to get full value for your planting dollars, however, you'll benefit from following as many of these rules as you can.

• Avoid buying rootbound plants. A plant should remain growing in a container only until its roots begin to fill the container. If you see a large plant you like growing in a suspiciously small container, ask if you can pop it out to examine its roots. If they are wrapping tightly around and around inside the container, don't buy—it's no bargain whatever the price. This is especially important with larger plants and trees, which will not anchor well into the soil in your yard if the growing roots choke each other. Poorly anchored trees are the first to fall over in high winds. If there is only minor root-wrapping, you can cut some of the outer roots with clippers to encourage better rooting.

• Plant at the right time of year. Fall, winter, and early spring are best for most plants. Winter is definitely the best time for planting bare-root plants—those with essentially no soil attached to the roots—provided the soil is not frozen when you plant. The plants will send out roots during all but the very coldest days in winter, and these roots will help them be more self-sufficient and better-established next summer. Bulbs planted in the fall put out enough root growth all winter to allow them to bloom their best in spring. You have probably noticed that mail-order nursery catalogs have cutoff dates for shipping certain kinds of plants. Your local nurseries can extend their selling seasons by offering plant material grown or planted in containers or balled and burlapped. This minimizes transplant shock for material you purchase in summer, but you should remember to give extra attention to watering your unseasonal buys.

Do not remove the burlap from around the rootball—unless, of course, the "burlap" is actually a non-rotting plastic fabric. If twine is used to wrap the top of the burlap around the trunk of the plant, cut that away, but leave the rest of the burlap on. It will help to stabilize the shrub or tree until it sends roots out into the surrounding soil.

• Prepare the soil properly. This may mean bringing in large quantities of organic soil amendment to mix in with the existing native soil. Ideally, as we discussed in Chapter 8, "Site Preparation," you should view soil preparation as something you do to an entire yard, not just to an individual planting hole. If you can't work on such a grand scale, then dig holes as large as you can and mix one part commercial topsoil mix or well-composted manure with two or three parts native soil. How large a hole is large enough? For annuals and perennials, dig a hole, say, 1 foot deep and 1 foot across, and for larger woody plants, twice as deep and broad. For trees, a hole 3 or 4 feet across and 3 feet deep would be adequate.

In any event, don't just pour a lot of topsoil or other soil amendment into the hole around the plant. Especially in very hard soils, you will end up with a bathtub effect—a plant in a pocket of good soil, surrounded by an impervious native soil. In wet weather, the pocket fills up with water and the plant can drown. Also, I know of numerous trees whose roots outgrew their pockets of rich soil but didn't extend out into the native soil, and the trees tipped over during fierce windstorms. It's discour-

aging to see, but easy to prevent: Remember to mix. If the existing soil is decent, you're better off in the long run planting directly into the native soil rather than surrounding the plant's roots in unmixed topsoil.

♦ Plant at the proper soil level. Gardeners east of the Cascades and in drier climates can safely follow traditional East Coast gardening wisdom, which says to place the crown of the rootball in a little depression below the level of the surrounding soil and to encircle the entire dripline with a little soil moat. This practice is designed to hold in precious water. In most places west of the Cascades, though, that advice is likely to drown plants when winter rains

1. Use a dolly for large plants. Mix one part topsoil, two parts native soil. 2. Position the plant. 3. Pack the mixed soil in well, soak the soil and rootball, and stake if needed.

one part topsoil

two parts native soil

moat for dry area

slope for wet area

staking detail

come. Professional landscapers west of the Cascades prefer to plant shallow, or to plant in raised berms, precisely to minimize the bathtub effect mentioned above in which water is trapped near the roots.

- Align plants properly. Many of the more rigid plants have a "front" and a "back" side because their leaves and branches have arrayed themselves to follow the sun; many, more lax plants, such as groundcovers, "flow" downhill. You can make an especially pleasing arrangement by facing all plants of a particular sort in the direction they would grow naturally: groundcovers all pointing downhill, with no rogue hill-climbers; shrubs facing uphill or toward paths, away from the shade of trees or taller bushes beyond. If one side of a shrub is leafier than the other, use the leafier side as its face.

- Water plants well as you install them, and pay special attention to watering them for at least the first growing season. One technique many landscapers use is to fill a wheelbarrow with a water-soluble fertilizer solution and soak the rootball of each plant before planting. The fertilizer should be a low- or non-nitrogen fertilizer, high in phosphorus and potash, to help stimulate quick, new root growth. Don't use high-nitrogen fertilizers because they will promote too much top growth before the plant has had a chance to get its roots established properly. For this reason, I don't recommend the use of fresh manure in the planting hole as a plant food. After the plant is in the ground, you will need to check

frequently to determine whether it needs water. For most new plantings, if you dig down two inches near the plant with a stick or a finger and find little or no sign of water, it's time to water. Of course, if a plant is showing signs of wilting leaves, then it's past time to water.

- After planting, cover the soil surface with a mulch. Ground bark is the standard mulch in the Northwest, where we admire its dark, earthy appearance and its long, useful life. Whether you use bark mulch, sawdust, or some other organic mulch, you will cut down your water requirements considerably. Two or three inches of mulch will help conserve soil moisture, reduce water runoff and soil erosion, and minimize weed problems. I like the idea of planting large quantities of low-growing groundcovers amid the larger plants, and then mulching only once, when the plantings are installed. As the groundcovers grow, less of the mulched area shows, and the visual need to freshen the mulch vanishes.

- Stake tall plants and trees if necessary. I don't automatically stake plants, because there is evidence that non-staked plants will establish themselves faster than staked plants. Still, tall trees or top-heavy plants in windy areas may benefit from temporary staking. For trees up to 6 or 8 feet high, two support posts, one on each side, should be enough. I prefer 2"x2" wood, up to 6 feet long. Other people use long reinforcing bars ("rebar"). Using a handsaw or a hatchet, cut a point on the bottom of each stake and use a sledge to pound the stakes in about 2 feet deep. Use wire or twine to tie the tree to both stakes. Where the wire curves around the trunk, sheath it with short lengths of rubber hose to protect the trunk. Don't fully encircle the trunk with a tight wrap of wire. Be sure that no wire or twine presses against the bark; cutting or abrasion could kill the plant. For larger trees that need an exceptional amount of support, use three guy wires instead of two posts, and peg the far ends with rebar, 2"x2"x18" pegs, or some of the commercially available soil anchors.

- Make a solemn vow to remove the stakes or guy wires within six to twelve months; write it on your calendar. If you forget to do this, the plants will suffer slow strangulation. It is not a pretty sight. I sometimes see situations where wire has cut deeply into the bark. When this happens, if the tree is not too badly damaged already, I will try to save it by unwrapping the wire as carefully as possible. If I'm not careful, I risk ripping off bark and damaging the plant instead of helping it. When the wire is thoroughly embedded in the bark, I use wire cutters to remove the wire I can reach safely, and ignore the rest, hoping that I've done enough.

Even some plant tags can have a tourniquet effect on branches and trunks. Although it can be difficult to keep track of everything in your garden, it shouldn't be too hard to have a planting plan that highlights the names and locations of the more substantial plants and trees in your yard. When you add something new, make a note of it on your plan.

Transplanting

What if you want to dig a plant out of one corner of your yard and plant it in another? I have dug and moved roses in July and large magnolias in May, and they have thrived despite their untimely moves—but I don't recommend that you try doing this before doing some careful planning first. Find out what the cost would be to simply buy a new plant of the same type and size, if one is available. That may be the sanest course.

If you truly want to keep a particular plant but it must be moved, and moved fast, you might want to risk doing an unseasonal transplant. Perhaps you have planned a new addition to your house and the bulldozer is waiting, or you are moving to a new house and want to take a few special plants with you. If you can wait until winter, when the plant approaches or enters dormancy, it will have a much better chance of survival. Even then, there is no absolute guarantee that a particular plant will live through a move. There are ways to increase your odds, though.

You will need to know whether the plants you want to move will tolerate being transplanted bare-root. Many deciduous shrubs and trees—those that lose their leaves in the wintertime—are good candidates. Roses and fruit trees are good examples. (These are the same plants you see for sale as bare-root plants in nurseries and garden centers. They are also the mainstay of mail-order nurseries that want to avoid the high costs of shipping plants with soil.) The only good time for you to dig and move these plants bare-root is when they are dormant, in the wintertime.

On the other hand, such plants as rhododendrons, most evergreens, dogwoods, and magnolias prefer to be dug with large rootballs intact. Many deciduous plants resent being bare-root after they have been planted for a few years. Even plants that tolerate being bare-root in winter often appreciate being moved with rootballs at other times of the year. Smaller plants have an easier time adapting to new environments than larger plants because they are less likely to have vital roots cut off in their uprooting.

MAKING THE MOVE: If you've made the decision to move a plant, you should begin by gathering the right tools and materials. For small plants, you can always use a wheelbarrow or wagon for transportation, but use a dolly with 8-inch-diameter wheels or larger for serious plant moves. Most rental shops carry these, and it is money well spent. It's too easy to damage your back lifting large shrubs into high wheelbarrows. (Dollies with smaller wheels are suitable only for carting things on walkways or steps, not over soft soil or lawns.) I also keep handy a small Swedish bow saw and long-handled loppers to clip large roots, handpruners for smaller roots, and an almost–flat-edged Danish spade for the actual digging. A spade works far better than the typical dished shovel, which is designed more for digging loose materials than for cutting through hard dirt and roots.

To move an extremely large plant, you need additional equipment: thick rope to pull the plant out of the digging hole, and extra horsepower to help with the pulling. The latter could include a come-along (a hand-powered winch), or a tractor, or a conveniently placed truck. The rope, incidentally, should be attached to the wrapped, secured rootball, never to the trunk of the plant. Wrapping a rope around the trunk and then pulling is very likely to damage or kill the plant. I prefer not to handle the plant by the trunk at all, for fear that the rootball will break loose from the trunk and ruin the plant's chances for survival.

Find plenty of burlap bags for your transplanting chores. The bags must not be made from plastic mesh; you are going to leave the burlap around the roots when you plant, and plastic mesh won't disintegrate in the soil. Years ago, potato sacks were made from a good grade of burlap, and you could pick up

◆

Smaller plants, being less likely to have vital roots cut off when uprooted, adapt more easily to a move than larger plants.

◆

plenty of burlap sacks cheaply and conveniently from grocery stores. Nowadays, most potato sacks are made from netted nylon mesh. If you live in a rural area, you could ask at a nearby feed store for burlap bags. In the city, your nursery might have them. Most nurseries either have treated burlap cloth cut to standard sizes or can direct you to appropriate suppliers. Treated burlap will last several months, which makes it particularly useful for plants that may not reach their permanent planting area for some time; eventually it disintegrates, allowing roots to grow through freely.

Have plenty of ungalvanized nails or sturdy twine nearby to hold the burlap bags together. (Galvanized nails don't slip between the burlap weave very gracefully.) Eight- to 16-penny flat-head nails should be satisfactory; use the larger nails for larger rootballs.

Dig the hole and prepare the soil where the plant will go before you dig up the plant itself. Prepare the soil you will use to fill in around the plant in its new hole just as you would for a new plant. (See "Planting," above.)

Wait for overcast, cool, or cloudy weather before you begin to dig. Although this advice is helpful for planting any plant, it is especially important for transplants. Water the plant a bit the day before. Don't soak the soil; that will make digging much harder when the soil turns to mud, and will increase the plant's weight considerably. You do want to keep the plant from drying out during the move, though.

Cut open the burlap sacks with a razor or knife so that they lie flat. If one sack will not wrap around the rootball of the plant you want to move, pin two or more burlaps together, using the ungalvanized nails. (Those of you who have had practice with diaper pins should have little difficulty with this.) If you use enough nails, the connected sacks should not come apart easily.

Many plants benefit from a top-pruning before they are moved. Since most plants are likely to lose at least some roots during transplanting, this will balance out the plants' water and nutrient requirements. Take the time to do some thoughtful pruning, not just a crew-cut.

If the plant you want to move has many low branches, carefully tie or wrap up the branches with burlap bags or polyethylene sheeting to keep them out of your way. You will especially appreciate this if your plant has stickers or thorns. Wrapping the branches is also helpful for long-distance moves in a car or truck; it will reduce dessication and wind damage caused by traveling at highway speeds.

Now you're ready to dig the plant. There is real skill involved in digging; many nurseries have crew members who specialize in digging plants so that the roots will hold together with the surrounding soil in a firm rootball. This is the key to success in transplanting. Obviously, nothing replaces practice, but using a few of their techniques and tricks can help you.

First, cut a circle of soil around the plant. Start big and work inward if you must. As with the making of a stone sculpture, it's hard to patch back on what's been chipped off. Try to make the rootball about 12 to 18 inches in diameter for every inch of trunk diameter. (Measure the trunk diameter at 12 inches above ground level; if it's more than 3 or 4 inches across, it's not a good candidate for a do-it-yourself move.) Don't try to pry the plant out. In soft soil, pretend that you are rowing with your spade. Reverse the blade of the spade so that it faces toward you and away from the plant. In hard soil, take the reversed blade and press it into the soil with your foot (or feet), and push straight down. Cut all the way around the plant in this fashion before you begin to remove any earth.

Next, keeping the spade facing away from the plant, make a trench on the outside of the circular cut you've already made. Dig the trench down 12 to 18 inches deeper if you still see major roots—before you begin to curve under to make the bottom of the ball.

If you don't see many roots, then you can gradually cut farther into the ball. You're trying to make a rootball, not a dirtball; extra dirt means extra weight, and could cause the rootball to break apart, which would harm the plant's chances of long-term survival.

Work to cut any remaining roots, including the taproot, underneath the ball. Use loppers to cut roots if you must.

When the rootball has been cut free, it will tell you. You shouldn't need to push on the trunk to force the plant over; a gentle push on the rootball should be enough.

Now it's time to wrap up. Fold the burlap around

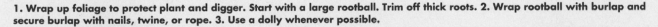

1. Wrap up foliage to protect plant and digger. Start with a large rootball. Trim off thick roots. 2. Wrap rootball with burlap and secure burlap with nails, twine, or rope. 3. Use a dolly whenever possible.

1   2   3

the rootball, as far as possible, then roll the ball back on top of the burlap and fold up the burlap around it the rest of the way. Use nails or twine to cinch the burlap tightly into place. If you're using nails, join the overlapped burlap edges together. Loose burlaps cause loose rootballs and unnecessary plant losses. If the plant or tree is very large, you will also want to make a rope sling around the rootball. The sling can be like a net surrounding the ball. Then tie your pulling rope, if any, to the sling—not to the trunk.

For a small to moderate-sized shrub (under 400 pounds), use a dolly as transport. I will often tie an awkward plant to the handles so it won't tip off at inopportune moments. A plant trussed up like this can be moved easily across any level or near-level stretch of land by two people. With plywood sheets or wooden planks, it can be moved almost vertically, even up rockeries or steps. Use a come-along winch tied to the handles of the dolly to give you additional stability and safety on slopes; even if you slip, the load will stay in place.

Carefully orient the plant in the proper direction and then tip it into its prepared hole. Water the plant well, soaking the rootball and any foliage, and fill in the soil around the ball. This is an ideal time to give the plant a half-strength dosage of soluble plant food mixed with the water. If you must move plants in early fall, use a non-nitrogenous fertilizer so that you don't promote fresh green growth just before winter. A fertilizer with plenty of potash and phosphorus will encourage new root growth and increase plant hardiness.

Pay special attention to watering needs through the plant's first growing season. This is especially important if you have moved the plant during its growing season. A plant moved while dormant is likely to grow new roots even in wintertime and early spring, which will help the plant pull more water from the soil in the warm days of summer. This gives it an advantage over a warm-season transplant with severed roots and a large spread of leaves transpiring water. Even drought-resistant plants are likely to need some supplemental watering for the first year or two after planting.

If you know in the wintertime that you will need to move a plant next summer, you can do some planning ahead that will increase your likelihood of success. You can dig a plant in the cold season and put it into a wooden box or pulp pot. Or, if you can't get a big enough container, you can do an in-place transplant now, followed by an actual move some months later. Landscapers call this process root-pruning. They will dig a plant most or all of the way out of the ground, then perhaps truss up the rootball in a treated burlap bag, and replant the plant in the same spot until moving time. They often use a mixture of native soil and bark or sawdust to fill in around the plant. If you have the time, early root-pruning and back-filling is an ideal method for ensuring high survivability of any large plants you want to move.

CHAPTER ELEVEN

Lawns

Sod and Seed,

Installation,

Reduced Maintenance

You may think that lawns are flat or gently sloping areas covered with grass. That's not really true. Most lawns are large black holes down which their owners dump amazing amounts of money, water, chemicals, fertilizers, and time, hoping to make their lawns look picture-perfect.

I don't know whether there is a technical name for this behavior, but certainly the advertising departments of the big fertilizer and chemical corporations are doing their best to encourage it.

Perhaps a lawn won't be the biggest expense in your yard at the outset. The costliest thing in the beginning could be a massive rockery, a deck or gazebo, a pool or patio. Or it could be a collection of large or rare shrubs or trees. But once those things are in place, they shouldn't require a great amount of upkeep. On a price-per-square-foot basis, your lawn could end up costing you much more in maintenance than any of the other items in your yard.

The bigger your lawn is, the more it will cost in terms of time, water, materials, and perhaps environmental damage.

That's too bad, because it doesn't have to be that way. There are some things you can do up front to minimize your costs in the times ahead. The first one, obviously, is to determine how much lawn you really need. The bigger your lawn is, the more it will cost to keep up: more time, more water, more materials, and possibly more environmental damage. Whatever you do to minimize the size of the lawn will work in your favor.

Lawns are wonderful for all kinds of outdoor play, and if you have children who need to let off energy, you may need a lawn; playing tackle football out in the street is not much fun. As the children grow up and use the lawn less, you can cut out larger and larger areas of it and convert them to flower beds, vegetable gardens, groundcovers, or paved areas.

Another way to effectively cut down on lawn size is to identify parts of your yard that aren't suited to grass, such as steep slopes and shady areas. Sloped lawns are hazardous to mow and encourage wasteful water runoff; shade compromises the lawn's health.

Water utilities in the maritime Pacific Northwest claim that people, in summertime, will use up to 50 percent of their household water trying to keep their lawns alive. People in drier parts of the region may use even more. Giving your lawn deep but less frequent waterings will encourage it to grow deeper roots, allowing it to survive better during periods of restricted water use. Of course, this holds true only for lawns with correctly prepared soil; the more ground preparation you do before planting the lawn, the less watering you will have to do. See the "Soil Preparation" section of Chapter 8 for some general guidelines.

Choosing the Lawn Type

I have seen leaflets from sod distributors that entice homeowners with promises of "lawns in a day." Don't believe it. You can lay pieces of sod over whatever soil you have in your yard, but I can't recommend it, unless you're one of the fortunate few who already have suitable soil conditions—or unless you're planning to sell your house in a few weeks and don't care what kind of headaches you leave to the future owner. Sod lawns, properly done, need exactly the same initial preparation as seed lawns, and it's not likely that both the preparation and laying of the sod for a typical lawn can be done in a single day.

So why should you choose one lawn type—sod or seed—over the other? The main reason for choosing sod is for the initial convenience—and you will pay for that convenience in time and the potential for problems in the future.

SOD: Consider these advantages and issues.
- A sod lawn will take less tending in the first weeks after it is installed. The surface of a seeded lawn must never dry out—and that may mean watering twice daily for at least two weeks.
- If the soil underneath is not too mushy, you can walk on a sod lawn immediately. With a seeded lawn, you risk scuffing or damaging the lawn seed as it sprouts. I know at least one family who chose sod because they wanted to have a wedding in the back yard, and there wasn't enough time for a seeded lawn to mature.
- Sod can be successfully installed any time the ground in your yard or at the sod farm is not frozen. West of the Cascades, this could be any month of the year. Seed, on the other hand, should be planted after the last frost in spring and well before the first

frost in fall; seed planted too late may not germinate until the following spring.

Many sod farms favor various bluegrass types, or cultivars, which do not do well west of the Cascades without massive amounts of assistance. The bluegrasses have roots that knit together well, making it easy to cut rolls or squares of sod. This is what makes them popular with sod farmers. The bluegrasses also tend to have a darker green color, which makes them easier to market because of their initial attractiveness. They are the lawn equivalent of Red Delicious apples, which look good in the produce bins but are boring to eat and, like the bluegrasses, grow better east of the Cascades. Most bluegrass cultivars are much more susceptible than other lawn varieties to rust, a lawn disease that can make large areas of grass turn a mottled orange and then die out. By and large, the bluegrasses also require larger quantities of fertilizer to keep their dark green color. And they absolutely will not thrive in shady places. Too often I see people spend a good deal of money for a sod lawn and then end up reseeding to make up for the shortcomings of the sod. Why not just use seed in the first place?

Beware of *Poa annua*, or annual bluegrass, a weed that often invades sod farms. Annual bluegrass has very light green foliage, which gives lawns an appalling checkerboard effect. It is pernicious because it sets seed and reinfests lawns no matter how low you cut the grass. Annual bluegrass is the nasty little secret of sod farms, some of which will sell off *Poa annua*–infested sections of sod for bargain prices. In some quarters, you will hear this weed called just "poa," which paints an entire genus as a villain when only one species has gone wrong.

An increasing number of sod farms grow sod containing a large percentage of perennial ryegrass. Older varieties of perennial ryegrass were disparaged because they gave a ragged edge when cut, but the newer perennial ryegrasses look very nice, and hold up better under less-than-ideal conditions. If you are considering sod instead of seed, perennial ryegrass would be a good choice. A few sod farms use fescue-type grasses. These will be harder to find, but are also worth considering.

SEED: Consider these advantages and issues.
- You are more likely to get the type of lawn most adapted to your part of the Pacific Northwest if you plant seed instead of sod.
- You can even tailor your lawn seeding to meet different needs in different parts of your yard, with shady lawn varieties for shady areas, sunny varieties for the brighter spots, and a mixture for the spots in between.
- The seed (and peat moss to cover) will be vastly less expensive than the sod, although most other preparation costs will be the same.
- For steep slopes that you don't intend to mow, but

that need a cheap plant cover for erosion control, you could consider hydroseeding. This is done by a service that sprays on a mixture of seed, fertilizer, and mulch to cling to the hillside until the seed sprouts. Most hydroseeding firms will let you choose from a variety of seed mixtures suitable to your needs; this could include different clovers or wildflower mixes.
- Consider hydroseeding as well for large areas where you want to install a more formal lawn. The only difference is that you might opt for a more expensive seed mix.

If you decide to plant a lawn from seed and you have the time and patience to get it started, you can choose from a much wider range of lawn types than sod shoppers can. You can vary the seed type from one part of the yard to another to take advantage of the strengths of each grass type. The grass seed companies know this, and market mixtures for different lawn needs. There is a good chance that you can find one or more prepackaged mixes that will fit your needs. I definitely recommend using a mixture over a single cultivar. Even if all reaches of your lawn have exactly the same sun exposure and soil, a mixture will give you better long-term results because you are spreading your bets.

So what should be in the mixture? I'll list some commonly recommended ingredients. Remember that within each genus of grass, there may be many species, each with its own strengths and weaknesses; and within each species, there may be many cultivars. Packages of seed are likely to have a description that implies their intended use, such as "playgrass" or "toughlawn" or "putting green," in big print on the label. But you will have to look for the much-smaller-type seed-content portion of the label to see the actual ingredients, which could include:

- **Perennial ryegrass.** This has many virtues—quickness of sprouting, good disease resistance, and generally lower fertilizer and chemical requirements. Named varieties are likely to give a smoother cut and have a finer blade than generic perennial ryegrass. If you want a permanent, evergreen lawn, avoid seed mixtures that contain *annual* ryegrass (or any other kind of annual grass), or you may find yourself with a sad-looking lawn come wintertime. For areas west of the Cascades, use up to 50 percent perennial ryegrass; it will also do well east of the mountains. I would suggest annual ryegrass only for casual-use areas.

- **Buffalo grass.** Weyerhaeuser has a new seed variety called "Watermiser" that looks promising; it sends roots far deeper into the soil than typical turfgrasses, so it can survive in periods of extended drought. It should be especially useful in drier climates, in areas where you don't need a highly groomed lawn.

- **Fescue.** Chewings fescue and creeping red fescue are fine-bladed contenders. You could use 10 percent or more in your mixture; creeping red fescue will work either on the east or west side of the Cascades.

- **Bentgrass.** You might consider highland colonial bentgrass, or some of its more recent relatives, but bentgrasses do cause some thatch buildup. Don't make it the primary ingredient in your lawn; 10 percent or so in a mix is fine.

- **Bluegrass.** *Poa pratens,* or Kentucky bluegrass, is one of the most beautiful of all lawns when properly maintained and grown in a suitable climate. It prefers a sunny exposure, lots of water and fertilizer, and a colder, drier winter than most of us get west of the Cascade mountains. East of the Cascades, it does very well indeed if properly tended; use 40 percent or more. Some newer cultivars of Kentucky bluegrass are more disease-resistant and less prone to problems than the traditional varieties, but Kentucky bluegrass is still not my turf of choice for areas west of the Cascades; keep it to 20 percent or less there.

If you have a shady area where you want to try to grow a lawn, you might try *Poa trivialis,* sometimes called shady bluegrass or rough bluegrass. It will persist much better in the shade than regular Kentucky bluegrass. You may have to call around to find sources for it. It is rarely available as part of a ready-made mixture; if you decide to use it, mix it by hand (30 percent or more) with other non-bluegrass cultivars before sowing. But remember that no grass type will thrive in dense shade. *There are limits to what you can do with lawns.* Shady areas might be good candidates for groundcovers or other lawn substitutes.

Preparing the Soil

Improve your soil before sowing seed or laying sod; it's hard to make soil changes once the lawn is done.

For the sake of your lawn's long-term health, you will have to prepare the soil before you sow seed or lay sod. It's the most effective time to help improve the soil; once the lawn is done, it's hard to make major changes. The suggestions below work well in the typical residential subdivisions west of the Cascades, where the native topsoil has been removed or obliterated by construction grading. For specifics on soil preparation, see that section in Chapter 8, "Site Preparation," or contact a soils expert.

After you have graded or leveled your lawn area, till the soil. You can use a tractor-tiller, a decent walk-behind tiller, or a shovel, but you must till the existing soil. Till 8 or more inches deep—the deeper the better.

Now it is time to add the organic material. This material could be sawdust, peat soil, peat moss, commercial or homemade compost, bark mulch, composted manure, or one of the commercial top-soil mixes. If you use a topsoil mix, ask your supplier what percentage of the mixture is organic matter. You should avoid bark or sawdust from Western red cedar, but most other trees make good sources. If you use fresh manure, you will need to wait a few weeks before actually laying down the sod or seed.

No matter what kind of organic material you use, the trick is to get enough and mix it in well enough. How much is enough? Tilling in 20 to 40 percent (20 percent for manure) would help greatly. A 4-inch layer, when tilled into the 8 inches of already-tilled existing soil, will give you 33 percent organic material ($4 + 8 = 12$, and $4 \div 12 = .33$). For every 1000 square feet (10'x100') you have, this means about 12 cubic yards of organic material. A 3-inch layer would require about 10 cubic yards. (If you want to be precise—which is not easy to do when spreading a big pile of stuff around—10 cubic yards = 270 cubic feet = 1080 square feet x 3 inches deep.) This would give you about 27 percent organic matter.

After spreading the soil amendment, till *again* to incorporate the new material with the existing soil. It's much better to till both before and after, rather than only after, you add the new material. If your soil test indicated that you should add nutrients, this would be a good time to do it; lawn food mixed into the soil is less likely to burn the grass and won't run off into the nearest storm sewer. And

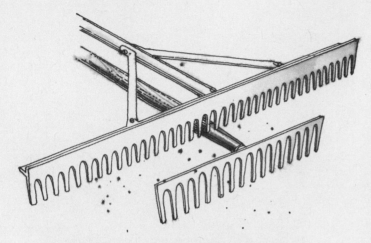

A wide magnesium or aluminum rake and a flat-head construction rake are ideal helpers for lawn-making.

if you are using bark mulch, sawdust, or another nitrogen-poor material, it is especially worthwhile to add some compensatory nitrogen before your second tilling.

The principle of double-tilling holds true even if you decide to add a topsoil mix instead of an organic soil amendment. Unless your soil is pure clay, don't just dump a layer of topsoil onto your existing dirt and then put a lawn on top of it. If you do, you will run afoul of the soil interface effect: the grass roots will work down through the good soil and stop when they reach the original soil. During the first hot, dry spell, you might start to see patches of droughty brown appear, no matter how often you are allowed to water. Once the water evaporates into the air or sinks through the first

few inches of good soil, it is no longer available to the grass roots.

Now get out a sturdy rake, a makeshift float, a shovel, a water roller, and a rock fork with strong tines and a sturdy handle. The rake could be an aluminum or magnesium rake, with a 3-foot-wide headful of tines. If you don't normally use such an oversized rake, consider renting one, instead. You could also use a regular steel garden rake, but not a bamboo or flexible-tine steel lawn rake. The float could be a 4'x4' pallet with a rope tied to it — a wooden pallet works just fine. You can also use a length of chain-link fence with about the same dimensions.

Use the float to level out the worst of the hills and dales from your lawn area; then use the rake for minor hand grading as needed. This is the very best time to get the lawn level! Give it your absolutely best effort now, and you won't have to struggle with it later. Go over the area several times if necessary. Remove any stones, sticks, or weed roots that you find, or they will come back to haunt you.

Check the level occasionally by stretching a string (with string level attached) over various points of the lawn bed. It might be helpful to use a shovel to dig out especially high areas and fill in especially low areas and then drag the float some more.

It's usually best not to have a perfectly flat lawn. Aim for a center slightly higher than the edges, or for a gentle slope from one corner to another. A 6-inch slope over a 20-foot stretch (5 percent grade) should be sufficient to help minimize swampy areas in the wintertime. If you can convince your lawn to slope away from your house, so much the better.

There are some definite tricks to using a float. If you cannot turn your float around after you reach one end of the lawn bed, the area may be too small to bother with a float. If there is enough area to warrant it, here's how to operate the float. While you face it, sling the rope on the outside of your arms and across your shoulders so that most of your upper body is supporting the effort of pulling the drag. Walk backward so that you can see what the float is doing. Experiment with speeding up and slowing down to see how to scrape material from high spots and deposit it in low spots. Periodically stop to pick out and remove any rocks, roots, and other debris that have been caught up by the float—there is no point in dragging it around. Add weights of rock or wood to hold down the float if it is not knocking down the high spots quickly enough.

A sod or brick pallet makes a good float or drag. Weight it down as needed.

Use a string and string level to check your lawn's slope.

But don't put so much weight on the float that you start to strain your body. If you pull muscles or get sunstroke doing this, you're doing something wrong.

When the lawn bed is quite smooth, set the float aside and begin with the rake. Treat your rake as if it were a household broom, not a hoe with teeth. Stand upright and sweep with the rake across the high spots, holding the rake vertically with the teeth parallel to the ground. Don't bend over and drag the rake or hack at the soil. Not only will it ruin your back for no good reason, but "hoeing" with a rake is likely to make divots in the lawn bed. If you find you still need to drag large volumes of soil, drag the float over the area again before continuing with the rake. If you need to drag small quantities of soil, flip the rake over and use the flat rather than tined side.

If your lawn area is over 3000 square feet, the area is probably too large for just a rake and a float, unless you really want the exercise or you don't have a big enough budget to afford my next suggestion: You may want to rent or hire a tractor with a rototiller and a built-in drag to grade, till, spread topsoil or soil amendment, till again, and float-level. If you have an especially rocky soil, you should also consider getting a power rock-rake to go over the area. This is a four-wheeled machine, about as big as a small tractor, with a modified scoop on the front. What do you do with all the rocks that get skimmed out of your soil? Use them as backfill behind a rockery or as the backbone of a mound or berm in the landscape. Or rinse them clean and use them to give a dry-streamed effect.

Once the soil is level, roll out the water roller. It usually makes more sense to rent one than buy one. Fill it with water to the point where you can comfortably roll it around. Use it to compress the tilled soil down a bit—just so it's not fluffy; you're not trying to compact it down to the density of cement. If this procedure reveals still-uneven spots in the lawn bed, use the rake and/or the float again. When the area is finally smooth to your satisfaction, rake the surface lightly one final time, just enough to roughen the surface. You are now ready to lay down sod or plant seed.

Lawn Edging

Before you install your lawn, take some time to determine how you are going to keep it in bounds. You could buy either a power edger or a half-moon edger, and make regularly scheduled edging runs. But you might be better off to put in some kind of physical barrier at the lawn's edge. Although it probably won't keep every blade of grass from invading your flower beds, it will substantially decrease the amount of continuing edging work you'll have to do.

You can install edging either before you make the lawn or after it is in and growing.

You can install edging either before you make the lawn or after it is in and growing. It is not a major project, compared to doing the actual lawn installation, and timing is not critical. Any of the following types of edging will work well.

- **Brick edging.** Brick adds a formal touch, with perhaps a European accent, to your landscaping. Use bricks laid flat, flush with the ground, not scallop-edged tiles or raised bricks laid on edge. (If your mower cannot straddle onto the brick, you'll have to pull out a weed trimmer to get the edges of the lawn to look tidy. In addition, people will trip over

Three good lawn edgers, plus one bad idea.

raised edging.) You can lay the brick end to end, for a narrow strip of edging, or side by side, for a more substantial edging. The bricks can go either in straight lines or in gentle curves—or both. Some grass will sneak through the gaps between the bricks, but this is not a major problem.

- **Wooden edging.** This kind of edging can add a civilizing touch to naturalistic Northwest landscapes. It is best done with 2"x4" or 4"x4" pressure-treated boards, laid flush with the ground. Obviously, this means the lawn's edges will be straight lines.

If you want curved wooden edging, you'll have to use 1"x4" material and kerf (make countless shallow cuts into) the inner side of the board so that it will bend more easily. This is excruciating work, and some of the boards you prepare will crack apart when you try to bend them into place. It can make you very humble. Avoid using thin bender board as a lawn edger in high-traffic areas. It does not hold up well over the years, and you will end up taking it out eventually. For less-traveled areas, knot-free cedar or redwood bender board may last a decade or two, especially if you double it up to give it some reinforcement.

- **Concrete edging.** Done either with a smooth finish or in exposed aggregate, concrete can be a superb edging for the lawn. Again, it should be flush with the lawn surface, not raised. It looks good either in straight lines or in curves. Concrete work is the least suitable for do-it-yourselfers.

- **Plastic or steel edging.** Over the past decade, these have had a great upsurge in popularity. Once in place, either material is almost invisible. Certainly the black plastic edging is far cheaper than steel, yet good-quality plastic edging—the sort with a solid bead on top and flanges to hold it in place—will give commendable service. At my first house, I installed some plastic edging that lasted without maintenance for over ten years. It looks best on informal curved edges because unrolling it into straight lines is difficult. I don't recommend using corrugated fiberglass or aluminum edging; fiberglass shreds and aluminum bends out of shape, and then they look appalling.

Any of these edging materials can also be used to contain gravel pathways. You should avoid placing any gravel or cobble walkways or streambeds next to your lawn. Some of the material will inevitably be scuffed or rolled over into the lawn area, where it will damage your mower blade and send stone missiles off in uncontrolled trajectories.

A final note: Don't flow your lawn right up into hedges, trees, or rockeries with the thought that you'll control things with a weed trimmer. That's just making more work for yourself, and the edge will never look as tidy as it should. Weed trimmers and lawn mowers are a major cause of tree damage.

Laying Sod

I'm assuming that you've already measured how many square feet of area you've prepared for your lawn. Since you will probably end up cutting off some small scraps on the edges as you do the final lawn shaping, consider ordering about 5 to 10 percent more sod than your estimated needs. Don't even order the sod until the ground is totally prepared. Sod on a pallet is

Alternating pattern for sod minimizes edge visibility.

like time-value mail; the longer it sits, the less it's worth. If the sod is delivered on a hot summer day, it can start to ferment even as you work; as you pull off piece after piece, the sod in the center gets hotter and hotter and turns into a very expensive instant compost pile. Sod left too long on the pallet will show visible signs of heat damage. It will have brownish or seared blades and may have a strong, composty odor. If the roots have not cooked too much, or if the color is merely on the yellow side, then it may recover after a while. If you think your sod is in danger of cooking, pull it off the pallet and lay it out flat—anywhere—as fast as you can. This will stop the composting process and save you a bundle of money. Do *not* soak hot sod rolled on the pallet; that will speed the composting process.

There is an important lesson in timing here. Have plenty of help on hand when the sod arrives; for large lawn areas (several thousand square feet or more), consider paying extra to have the sod delivered in smaller quantities spread out over several days or weekends. An experienced solo layer can lay out and trim a thousand square feet in two or three hours; it might take you more time until you get up to speed. Don't expect much sympathy from the sod company if you've neglected to have sufficient help on hand to lay the sod.

Sod delivered in the cooler season, from October through April, can perhaps sit safely for a day or longer without damage. The cooler the weather, the longer the sod can sit. Don't let this lull you into inactivity, though.

If you have several pallets of sod to lay, try to get the delivery people to place the pallets in a line or lines along the side(s) of your lawn bed, rather than in a cluster next to the street. (Do this only if you're willing to sign a damage waiver in case the sod truck's forklift damages your driveway or sidewalk.) This will decrease the distance you will have to haul the sod from pallet to placement, and will minimize foot damage to the careful grading and leveling you have done.

I prefer to start on the lowest edge, when possible, and work uphill. This allows me to pressure-fit higher rows against the rows below. Sod will sometimes seem to shrink at the edges a few days after it has been laid; the tighter you push the pieces together when you start, the less the seams will show. Stagger the rows so that edges don't line up; this will make the sod look more like a mature lawn faster.

Once the sod is laid, use a lawn edger or half-moon edger to trim the edges of the lawn to the shape you want. If the soil is very soft from the tilling, you might want to wait a week or so before cutting off the edge scraps so that the soil has a chance to settle.

Water the sod generously when you are finished—enough to wet the sod itself and the soil beneath for 2 to 3 inches. For the next two weeks, do a twice-daily moisture check: Lift up the edges of various pieces of sod to see if the soil underneath is damp. If it is approaching dryness, haul out the sprinkler. You don't need to soak it to the point of mushiness. Early morning is the best time to water. Try not to water in the afternoon or evening if you can avoid it—although if the lawn is dry, you'll have to get some water to it, regardless of the time.

Sowing Seed

If you have decided to go with seed, you are excused if you feel a bit smug. Although the initial preparation steps are the same, from this point on you are saving money. If you decide to have a hydroseeding firm apply the seed and protective mulch, you can skip down to the section below on keeping your lawn seed moist. Otherwise, choose a seed type or mixture according to your specific needs as mentioned earlier in this chapter. Read the label to determine how much area the package will cover. Measure the length and width of the area you wish to seed, and buy what you need plus a little extra—to help fill in any obvious bare spots where seed doesn't sprout due to washouts from rain or poor watering practices, or to help you repair damaged areas after the lawn has become established. With seed mixes, it helps to reblend all the seed in the package before you start, in case one seed variety has settled to the bottom.

Whirlybird for spreading seed.

You will need some kind of mechanical seed broadcaster. This can be a simple whirlybird spreader with a crank handle, or a drop-type spreader that you can later use to spread fertilizer as well. I can guarantee that you will have to do some experimenting to determine the best rate of coverage; lawn seed types vary greatly in size, and spreaders may not be calibrated very scientifically. It's best with seed, as with fertilizers, to spread the material lightly in a crisscross fashion, rather than heavily in a unidirectional pattern. This will give you more even coverage and you will avoid or minimize thick and thin alternations.

You will also need dry, fine-grind baled peat moss, at the rate of 8 cubic feet per 1000 square feet of lawn, plus a peat spreader. Peat spreaders are designed to lay a thin, even protective cover of peat over the seed, to protect it from depredations by birds, washouts, and drought until the lawn becomes established. I have never managed to do a decent, even job of spreading peat by hand. Peat spreaders are available from rental shops, or sometimes you can rent or borrow them from

SOME ALTERNATIVES TO LAWN

MOST OF THE ABOVE information assumes that you want to have a first-rate lawn, that you are willing to take the time to do it right, and that you can afford it too. But if you are on a limited budget, or if you aren't looking for perfection, you might get acceptable results with less effort. This could mean doing less preliminary soil work, adding less soil amendment or none at all, or going with a utility seed mix instead of special turf mixes.

If your primary goal is to prevent erosion from wind or water, a mix that contains clover could be a good choice, although this may sound strange to anyone who has tried to battle clover in fancier lawns. Because clover is nitrogen-fixing, you won't have to fertilize it.

If you simply want something to cover the soil, and you don't intend to walk in the area very much, then your options could include choosing from a wide variety of groundcovers. Many groundcovers never need mowing; others need mowing only once a year or so. You will be applying a lot less fertilizer than for lawn, and less frequently too. And many groundcovers will happily survive those occasional droughts that will quickly brown out even the best-defended turf lawns. Look through three separate lists of suggested groundcovers at the end of this book—in the "Edible Plants," "Drought-Resistant Plants," and "Native Plants" sections of the Appendix. Your water department will thank you if you do.

nurseries that sell peat moss.

If you live in a very windy area, peat moss is likely to blow away before it does much good. You'll have better success if you cover the seed with sawdust.

After you have sown the seed and laid the peat moss or sawdust, it is time to start watering. You need a sprinkler that will emit a fine, even spray, rather than large water droplets which can displace the seed. Once you start watering, you must not let the peat-moss seed cover dry out until the seed has sprouted and become reasonably well established. If you let germinating lawn seed dry out before it has a chance to send roots down into the soil, it will die, and you will have to re-seed and repeat the dry areas.

Peat moss spreader.

How much watering will you need to do? Use the color of the peat moss as a guide: It should always be dark and damp, never light and dry. If the weather does not provide enough moisture to keep the surface of the peat darkened, then you need to turn on the sprinkler. This is one of the few instances in which frequent, light waterings are actually better than infrequent, deep waterings. If you apply too much water, the seed and peat are likely to lift up and float away downhill, or rearrange into interesting, rippling patterns of thick green and barren brown. When it becomes clear that you do need to supply more water, try to do it in the early morning or at least before noon. Avoid late-evening waterings when you can, since that can increase the chance of fungal infection and slow germination by cooling the seed—but don't let that stop you if the lawn is drying out.

You will have to show great patience; although perennial ryegrass seed may start sprouting within seven to ten days, other types of turf seed may not make a real showing for two to three weeks. Continue the frequent watering until there is a good stand of lawn showing and you are ready to do the first mowing. This means that if you don't have an automatic watering system which you can set for short, multiple waterings each day, you will have to baby-sit the lawn until it becomes established. Either you or someone you trust will have to delay vacation plans for the time being.

Once the lawn is up and running, you can gradually lengthen the time between waterings. Within two months after seeding, you should be able to decrease the waterings to early morning, every other day or every third day in the summertime, and less frequently in other seasons. Your lawn won't be droughtproof, but it should stand up to much more drought than less-prepared turf in the neighborhood.

CHAPTER TWELVE

A Look to the Future

Stewardship of the Land

$\mathcal{T}$he process of landscaping has three parts—design, construction, and maintenance. Together, they make up the life cycle of the landscape. In this book, we've concentrated on the first two steps as they apply to home landscaping.

Any attention you give to the planning and implementation stages will make the maintenance stage easier for you. But your landscape and your life are dynamic events. Treat your landscape plan as a general guide, rather than a rigid commandment that you must observe. Things change. Plants grow, or sometimes perish. Your interests may shift over the years. It's good to take stock of your garden situation occasionally to make sure that it still meets your needs. You might want to reread portions of this book to help you measure how well your plan still stacks up. When you do, I hope you will also measure the predictions that follow for accuracy.

Prognostication is always a risky business; just look through some old science fiction magazines or urban-planning reports, and compare their visions with where we are today. Remember the promise (or was it a threat?) in the fifties that we would have atomic-powered hovercars by the nineties, making freeways obsolete? Still, I think we can make some predictions about certain trends in landscaping:

- The population of the Northwest will rise, while the amount of available piped water will remain at best constant—which means there will be less water to go around for "frivolous" uses such as lawns and landscape plants. Joshua is standing before the gates of Jericho, and he's carrying a water bill in his hand. Water-wise gardening, incorporating drought-resistant plantings, will become increasingly important.

- The supply of bark mulch and sawdust, which are byproducts of the lumber industry, will shrink as Northwest lumber mills slow down or stop production in response to economic shifts and restrictions on timber cutting. Prices for the wood we use in fences, timber walls, and decks will go up as the supply shrinks, and will rise even more rapidly after British Columbia is completely clear-cut. The available wood won't look as good, either. Expect to find more knotholes and a relaxing of standards in wood grading.

- Compost made from recycled yard waste (which is just now going into commercial production) and sludge (which is already being used for some mixes) will ease the pain of topsoil mix and bark mulch prices. It will increasingly become a part of soil mixes, and could provide an alternative to the use of bark in landscaping. I think that using these materials in ornamental plantings is far superior to the alternative, which is to dump all this material in a landfill and hope it goes away.

- Expect to see an increase in the use of various types of textured concrete or recycled plastic building blocks for retaining walls. They will become economically more attractive as wood prices push upward. And who knows? Perhaps we will eventually use recycled plastic planks for decks and fences.

- Pesticide use will shift as old standbys are banned or restricted and fewer new chemicals pop up to replace them. Organic methods of pest control will continue their migration into the mainstream as big companies smell money in the "green" trend. But because organic pest control requires some expenditure of effort and thought if it is to work properly, and because it lacks the quality of instant gratification, many people will yearn for the "good old days" of chemicals. Some truly useful and environmentally safe new chemical pesticides may not make it onto the market because of the extremely high cost of testing and certifying new pesticides.

- Lot sizes will continue to shrink, and increasing numbers of people will find that their dreams of a large lawn have become impractical.

- Fewer of us will be able to afford to buy housing anywhere near our workplaces, and longer commutes will mean less available time for yard upkeep.

- Landscaping styles from even more cultures will enrich the Northwest's already diverse palette. In step with the trend toward drought-resistant plantings will be the adoption of planting styles—not just plants—from the Mediterranean, northern Africa, and Australia. We will experience some moments of disequilibrium until we become accustomed to these newcomers. Chinese landscaping, with its own unique flavor, will come calling, providing a more structured alternative to Japanese landscaping.

I am acutely aware, as I sit in my suburban home surrounded by my family, that all of us live in a privileged moment in time. I hope that even our children and grandchildren will be able to afford a house and a patch of land, and will not have to live in concrete and plasterboard warrens. But I know that there is only so much room to go around. Those of you who live east of the mountains or out in the more rustic sections may have a hard time picturing this, until the farm next door turns into a subdivision for people who commute 60 or 80 miles away to the city.

That's what's happening and will continue to happen. Regional governments are struggling with these issues right now: Should they encourage higher-density land use by legislating open space? Or should they let the market rule development and let tract after tract of wilderness fall to the encroachment of the suburbs?

It's a dilemma for which there is no ready remedy. Perhaps part of the answer lies in the concept of stewardship. We guide and manage the treasures of the land not only for our own benefit but for the benefit of those to come. As I wrote this book, I came in touch with a number of people who have something of that long view. I've seen this process at work in many people, but I know it needs nurturing. Landscaping your own home will help you learn something about plants, trees, and soil. By nurturing the land, we can nurture ourselves. I invite you to get a shovel and start digging. Get to know your nearest neighbor, the earth.

Landscape Plant Lists

The following pages offer lists of several landscape plant groups: edible plants, poisonous plants, those that are drought-resistant, and those native to the Northwest.

I've organized the plants within each group according to their landscape uses: trees, shrubs, vines, groundcovers, vegetables, herbs, and flowers. Some plants could overlap into several categories. Most are listed alphabetically by botanical name, with common name in parentheses. An **E** or **W** accompanies plant types more suitable for growing on either the east or the west side of the Cascade mountains. These lists are not intended to be exhaustive, but I hope they prove a useful starting point.

Edible Plants

There are many obvious choices for landscape-worthy plants that produce edible crops, and a few less-obvious choices as well. Some, such as madrona (*Arbutus Menziesii*) and daylily (*Hemerocallis* spp.) are less obvious because we don't normally recognize what they produce as being edible, so you may want to try them in a suitable recipe before putting them in your yard—or leave their bounty as forage for the local wildlife. Some plants, such as barberry (*Berberis* spp.) and Oregon grape (*Mahonia* spp.) are edible but are not by any measure delicious. Still others may have crops that are clearly edible, but may not be considered attractive landscaping plantings. Some people, for example, like salmonberry and thimbleberry (*Rubus* spp.) in the right setting, while others consider them to be weeds. If you don't like the look of a plant, you'll have to like the crop in order to make planting it worthwhile. If you are interested in creating a wildlife sanctuary in your yard, this list of edible plants should be of particular interest. There is a lot of overlap between what people eat and what birds and other creatures eat.

If you have a strong interest in incorporating edible plants into your garden, be sure to look into at least these two books: *Designing and Maintaining Your Edible Landscape Naturally*, by Robert Kourik (Metamorphic Press/Rodale, 1986) and *Complete Book of Edible Landscaping*, by Rosalind Creasy (Sierra Club Press, 1982). For a well-researched look into native edible plants, please see Janice J. Schofield's *Discovering Wild Plants: Alaska, Western Canada, the Northwest* (Alaska Northwest Books, 1989).

I have purposely left a few "edible" plants, such as comfrey (*Symphytum*), Sassafras, and labrador tea (*Ledum* spp.), out of this list because of questions about their long-term safety—they all contain naturally occurring toxins.

Not all parts of "edible" plants are necessarily edible. Certainly you wouldn't want to eat rhubarb leaves or cherry leaves. Be very careful about allowing children to harvest anything from your yard without your direct supervision. If they see you sampling unusual-looking foodstuffs from the yard, they may interpret it as permission for them to do the same with anything that looks remotely interesting. A selected list of poisonous plants follows the list of edible plants. Unless otherwise indicated in the lists below, *the edible part of the plant is the fruit.*

TREES

Arbutus Menziesii (madrona, arbutus) **w**

Asimina triloba (pawpaw) **w**

Castanea spp. (chestnut)

Cornus spp. (dogwood)

   kousa (kousa dogwood)

   mas (cornelian cherry, yellow-flowered dogwood)

Corylus spp. (filbert, hazelnut)

Crataegus (hawthorn—the following are good for jams/jellies)

   azarolus (azarole)

   Douglasii (black hawthorn)

   lobulata

   mollis (downy hawthorn)

Cydonia oblonga (fruiting quince)

Diospyros virginiana (American persimmon) **w**

Ficus carica (fig) **w**

Ginkgo biloba (maidenhair tree; seed "nut" edible, but fruit is smelly)

Juglans regia (walnut)

Malus spp. (apple and crabapple)

Mespilus germanica (medlar—excellent ornamental, use fruit in jams)

Prunus spp. (cherry, peach, plum, prune, almond)

Punica granatum (pomegranate) **w**

Pyrus spp. and hybrids (pear, Asian pear)

Rhamnus purshiana (cascara—bark used as a laxative)

Tilia spp. (linden—flowers for tea)

SHRUBS

Amelanchier spp. (serviceberry)

Arbutus unedo (strawberry tree) **w**

Berberis spp. (barberry)

Chaenomeles (flowering quince)

Mahonia aquifolium (Oregon grape)

Ribes (gooseberry, currant)

Rosa (rose—seed hips are edible)

Rubus

   idaeus (raspberry)

   parviflorus (thimbleberry)

   spectabilis (salmonberry)

Vaccinium

   corymbosum (blueberry)

   ovatum (evergreen huckleberry) **w**

   parvifolium (red huckleberry)

VINES

Actinidia chinensis and other spp. (kiwi vine) **w**

Akebia quinata

Passiflora caerulea, P. incarnata (passionflower) **w**

Rosa spp. (climbing roses)

Rubus spp. (blackberry, tayberry, marionberry, boysenberry)

Vitis (grape)

GROUNDCOVERS

Arctostaphylos

   x *media*

   uva-ursi (kinnikinnick)

Fragaria spp. (strawberry)

Gaultheria procumbens (wintergreen)

Mahonia nervosa (Cascade Oregon grape)

Mentha requienii (Corsican mint)

Thymus (thyme)

Vaccinium

   macrocarpon (cranberry)

   vitis-idaea (lingonberry)

VEGETABLES

(bean, pea, and tomato vines are especially useful as quick temporary covers for wire fences)

Artichoke **w**

Asparagus

Beans

Cabbage

Coltsfoot, Japanese (*Petasites japonicus*)

Kale, flowering

Lettuce (especially red-leafed varieties)

Peas

Rhubarb (stalks only)

Seakale (*Crambe maritime*)

Tomato

HERBS

Angelica

Anthriscus cerefolium (chervil)

Atriplex hortensis (orach)

Chrysanthemum parthenium (feverfew)

Foeniculum vulgare (fennel)

Lavandula spp. (lavender)

Levisticum officinale (lovage)

Mentha spp. (mint)

Myrrhis odorata (sweet cicely)

Ocimum basilicum (basil)

Origanum spp. (oregano)

Petroselinum crispum (parsley)

Salvia spp. (sage)

FLOWERS

Aster spp.

Bellis perennis (English daisy)

Chrysanthemum spp.

Cosmos spp.

Crocus sativus (the red stigmata are true saffron)

Dahlia spp.

Helianthus tuberosus (roots are edible)

Hemerocallis (daylily—all parts are edible)

Primula (including primrose)
polyanthus
vulgaris

Tropaeolum majus (nasturtium)

Viola
cornuta (violet)
wittrockiana (pansy)

Poisonous Plants

No listing of edible plants is complete without a quick look at the other side. Here are some of the more obvious toxic plants. The safest approach is to assume that all plants are poisonous until positively identified, and to indoctrinate this into young children.

Aconitum spp. (monkshood, wolfsbane)

Actaea rubra (baneberry, chinaberry)

Colchicum spp. (meadow saffron)

Convallaria majalis (lily-of-the-valley)

Daphne spp. **w**

Delphinium elatum

Digitalis spp. (foxglove)

Hedera spp. (ivy)

Hyacinth spp.

Kalmia spp.

Narcissus spp. (daffodils, jonquils, narcissus)

Pieris spp.

Prunus laurocerasus (English laurel) **w**

Rhododendron spp. and hybrids **w**

Taxus spp. (yew)

Drought-Resistant Plants

You can call it xeriscaping, or you can call it drought-resistant landscaping; either way, this kind of approach to landscaping your yard can make a lot of sense. Even in the rainy Pacific Northwest, water utilities are beginning to encourage water conservation as regional water supplies become more uncertain. Water shortages occur because of population growth and because we are dependent upon sufficient mountain snowfall in the wintertime to provide enough water to get by during the summertime. If the snow fails to materialize, we go on water rationing. While I don't expect that water restrictions will become as severe in the Pacific Northwest as in parts of drought-burdened California, certainly the problem won't go away. It will only get worse as the population and demands on water resources increase and the supply—at best—remains constant.

The first step you can take is to keep lawn size to a minimum in your yard. On a gallon-per-square-foot basis, lawns will need more water than anything else you could plant, except maybe water lilies. If you decide that you do need a lawn, place it where it will do the most good—perhaps in a highly visible spot or as a wide pathway through planting areas. Look to Chapter 11, "Lawns," for guidance in preparing a lawn that will require the least amount of water. (Then, for some amusement, read the section of Thorstein Veblen's classic *Theory of the Leisure Class* in which he describes why we have lawns at all.)

The next step is to use water as cleverly as possible. This means supplying water with pinpoint accuracy, rather than broadcasting it far and wide into corners where it isn't needed. (Look to the section on irrigation in Chapter 8, "Site Preparation," for more information.) It could also mean grouping plants with similar water needs together: drought-resistant plants with drought-resistant plants, and water-loving plants with water-loving plants. This will make your caretaking easier, too.

The last step is to make sure that as many plants in your yard will be as drought-resistant as possible. Here are some possibilities:

- Plants that are native to our area (or similar areas) and thus are adapted to the rainy winter/dry summer pattern typical here. (Of course, this does not include native swamp or wetland plants.)
- Plants from low-rainfall areas that prefer dry summers but can tolerate our wet winters.

- Plants that normally prefer a generous amount of summer water, but can tolerate a diminished supply of water when *absolutely* necessary, after they are *well established*, and when they are planted in *properly prepared* soil. This category can even include rhododendrons and azaleas, except those planted in the shade of especially thirsty trees.
- Plants which go dormant during summer. As you might expect, this includes many of our spring-flowering bulbs, and some of our best-loved perennials.

What follows is a list of plants which are, with a little help from you, adaptable to low-water conditions in your yard. Please note that some genera of plants, and even some species within a particular genus, will tolerate more drought than others. An asterisk (*) denotes native plants. I hope you can see from the wide variety of plants listed that working with real or potential water restrictions doesn't automatically limit us to arid-looking landscapes. I do not think that every yard must look as if it sprang full-blown from the deserts of southern California. Instead, look over the range of plant materials in the list below and incorporate those that will fit into the vision you have of your garden.

CONIFEROUS TREES

Calocedrus decurrens (incense cedar)
Cedrus
   atlantica (Atlas cedar) w
   deodara (deodar cedar) w
   libani (cedar of Lebanon) w
x *Cupressocyparis Leylandii*
   (Leyland cypress)
Juniperus (juniper)
   chinensis 'Keteleeri'

   (Keteleer juniper)
   *occidentalis** (Western juniper)
   scopulorum 'Pathfinder'
   virginiana 'Cupressifolia,' 'Skyrocket'
Pinus (pine)
   *attenuata** (knobcone pine)
   Coulteri (Coulter pine)
   edulis (pinon pine)
   *Jeffreyi** (Jeffrey pine)
   mugo rostrata

   peuce (Macedonian pine)
   pinea (Italian stone pine) w
   *ponderosa** (Western yellow pine)
   sabiniana (digger pine) w
Taxodium
   distichum (bald cypress—tolerates extremely wet soil, too)
   mucronatum (Montezuma cypress) w
*Thuja plicata** (Western red cedar)

BROAD-LEAFED TREES

Albizia julibrissin (silk tree)

Arbutus Menziesii (madrona, arbutus) **w**

Crataegus (hawthorn—many species)

Ficus carica (fig)

Gleditsia triacanthos (honey locust)

Juglans spp. (walnut)

Koelreuteria paniculata (goldenrain tree)

Malus (crabapples—many species— most tolerate wet soil too)

Morus spp. (mulberry)

Populus spp. (Are you sure you want a poplar?)

Prunus spp. (upright flowering cherries)

Quercus (oak)
  coccinea (scarlet oak)
  *Garryana** (Garry oak)
  robur (English oak)

Robinia pseudoacacia (black locust)

Tilia spp. (linden)

*Umbellularia californica** (Oregon myrtle, California bay) **w**

SHRUBS

Abelia
  grandiflora **w**
  g. 'Edward Goucher' **w**

*Amelanchier** spp. (serviceberry)

Arbutus unedo (strawberry tree) **w**

*Arctostaphylos**
  columbiana (hairy manzanita) **w**
  manzanita (common manzanita) **w**

Aucuba japonica **w**

Berberis spp. (barberry)

Buddleia
  alternifolia (fountain butterfly bush)
  Davidii (butterfly bush)

*Ceanothus**
  thyrsifolius (blueblossom) **w**
  velutinus (deer brush)

Chaenomeles spp. (flowering quince)

Cistus spp. (rockrose) **w**

Cotinus coggygria (smoke tree)

Cotoneaster (taller species) **w** (some hardy **E**)

Deutzia spp.

Elaeagnus spp. (silverberry)

Escallonia spp. **w**

Fatsia japonica **w**

Forsythia spp.

*Garrya elliptica** (silk tassel) **w**

Hamamelis spp. (witch-hazel)

Hibiscus syriacus (rose of Sharon)

*Holodiscus discolor** (ocean spray)

Juniperus communis (common juniper varieties)

*Mahonia aquifolium** (Oregon grape)

Nandina domestica (heavenly bamboo)

Osmanthus spp. **w**

*Philadelphus Lewisii** (mock orange)

Pinus mugo (mugho pine)

Prunus lusitanica (Portuguese laurel) **w**

Pyracantha spp. (firethorn) **w**

Rhamnus spp. (buckthorn, but not cascara)

*Rhus** spp. (sumac)

*Ribes sanguineum** (red-flowering currant)

Rosa (old-fashioned and shrub roses, *not* hybrid tea roses)

Rosmarinus spp. (rosemary) **w**

Tamarix spp. (tamarisk)

Taxus spp. (yew)

Vaccinium ovatum (evergreen or saltwater huckleberry) **w**

VINES

Campsis radicans (scarlet trumpet)

Clematis texensis (scarlet clematis)

Cobaea scandens (cup-and-saucer vine—annual)

Euonymus fortunei **w**

Hedera helix (English ivy)

Polygonum Aubertii (silver lace vine)

Rosa (old climbing roses)

Wisteria spp.

GROUNDCOVERS

(woody and herbaceous)

Anacyclus depressus (Mt. Atlas daisy)

*Arctostaphylos**
  x *media*
  uva-ursi (kinnikinnick)

Caryopteris clandonensis (blue mist)

*Ceanothus gloriosus** (Point Reyes ceanothus) **w**

Cotoneaster (lower-growing species and cultivars) (some hardy E)

Dryas* spp. (mountain avens)

Genista (creeping brooms)
  lydia
  pilosa
  sagittalis (arrow broom)

Gypsophila repens (creeping baby's breath)

Juniperus (lower-growing species)

Mahonia nervosa* (Cascade Oregon grape)

Penstemon* (beard tongue)
  Davidsonii
  pinifolius

Potentilla tabernaemontanii (spring cinquefoil)

Sedum spp.

Thymus spp. (thyme)

Vinca minor (periwinkle)

PERENNIALS, BULBS, AND ANNUALS

Achillea spp. (yarrow)

Arabis spp. (rockcress)

Armeria maritima (thrift)

Artemisia spp. (wormwood, dusty miller)

Aurinia saxatilis (basket-of-gold — also known as Allysum)

Baptisia australis (wild indigo)

Calendula officinalis (pot marigold)

Centranthus ruber (red valerian)

Cerastium tomentosum (snow-in-summer)

Cleome spinosa (spider plant)

Coreopsis spp. (tickweed)

Cortaderia selloana (pampas grass) w

Cosmos spp.

Crocosmia crocosmiiflora (montbretia)

Dianthus spp. (pinks, carnations)

Dicentra formosa (bleeding heart)

Dictamnus albus (gas plant)

Echinops exaltatus (globe thistle)

Eremurus spp. (desert candle)

Eriogonum spp. (buckwheat)

Euphorbia spp. (spurge)

Gaillardia (blanket flower)

Gazania spp.

Hemerocallis spp. (daylily)

Iberis gibraltarica (Gibraltar candytuft)

Iris*
  Douglasiana
  tenax

Kniphofia (red-hot poker)

Lavandula spp. (lavender)

Linum spp. (flax)

Mirabilis jalapa (four o'clocks)

Narcissus spp. (including daffodils)

Oenothera spp. (evening primrose)

Papaver orientalis (Oriental poppy)

Pennisetum setaceum (fountain grass)

Petunia spp.

Phlomis fruticosa (Jerusalem sage)

Phlox spp.

Phormium (New Zealand flax) w

Portulaca spp. (rose moss)

Romneya Coulteri (Matilija poppy)

Rudbeckia hirta (gloriosa daisy)

Santolina
  chamaecyparissus (Lavender cotton)
  virens

Salvia spp. (sage)

Tithonia rotundifolia (Mexican sun-flower)

Verbena spp.

Yucca spp.

Native Plants

Dozens of plants native to our area make excellent choices for a wide range of landscape styles—ranging from the obvious native-Northwest to formal, even classical, European. Some of these plants are so widely used in the nursery trade that you might not even realize that they do come from our area originally. Others may have more modest charms or more exacting environmental needs that limit their usefulness to a few specific settings, perhaps in a less-developed woodland, wetland, or meadow garden. An asterisk (*) denotes those trees, shrubs, and herbaceous plants that are commonly considered to have the greatest merit for the widest range of gardens. The plants not asterisked could be of interest to you if you seek to build up a native plant collection or have other needs which match a given plant's uses.

For our purposes here, I am using the term "native" to encompass British Columbia, Washington, Oregon, and western Idaho. This area includes an extremely wide range of climates and ecosystems, from relatively mild coastal temperatures to harsh weather extremes; from shoreline to alpine, from rainforest to near-desert. In most cases, plants from the harsher environments will adapt well enough to the milder coastal climate, although you may need to pay special attention to soil drainage. Unfortunately, plants from milder regions don't always thrive east of the Cascades.

Two important works for people interested in more details about native plants are Arthur R. Kruckeberg's *Gardening with Native Plants of the Pacific Northwest* (University of Washington Press, 1982) and Janice J. Schofield's *Discovering Wild Plants: Alaska, Western Canada, the Northwest* (Alaska Northwest Books, 1989).

CONIFEROUS TREES

Abies (fir)
  amabilis (silver fir)
  grandis (grand fir)
  *lasiocarpa** (alpine fir)
  procera (noble fir) **w**
*Calocedrus decurrens** (incense cedar)
Chamaecyparis
  *Lawsoniana** (Lawson cypress, Port Orford cedar) **w**
  *nootkatensis** (Alaska cedar) **w**
Juniperus (juniper)
  occidentalis (Western juniper)
  scopulorum (Rocky Mountain juniper)

Larix occidentalis (Western larch)
Picea (spruce)
  Brewerana (Brewer's spruce) **w**
  Engelmannii (Englemann spruce)
  sitchensis (Sitka spruce) **w**
Pinus (pine)
  albicaulis (whitebark pine)
  attenuata (knobcone pine)
  *contorta** (lodgepole pine, shore pine)
  monticola (Western white pine)
  ponderosa (yellow pine)
*Pseudotsuga Menziesii** (Douglas fir)
Sequoia sempervirens (redwood) **w**
Taxus brevifolia (Western yew)

*Thuja plicata** (Western red cedar)
Tsuga (hemlock)
  *heterophylla** (Western hemlock)
  *Mertensiana** (mountain hemlock)

BROAD-LEAFED TREES

Acer (maple)
  *circinatum** (vine maple)
  *glabrum Douglasii** (Douglas maple, Rocky Mountain maple) **E**
  macrophyllum (bigleaf maple) **w**
Alnus rubra (red alder—only for wilder woodscapes) **w**
*Arbutus Menziesii**(madrona, arbutus—beautiful but temperamental) **w**

Betula (birch)
  occidentalis (red birch) **E**
  papyrifera (paper birch)
Chrysolepis chrysophylla (golden
  chinquapin) **w**
Cornus Nuttalli *(Pacific dogwood—
  beautiful but vulnerable to disease)
Crataegus Douglasii (black hawthorn)
Fraxinus latifolia (Oregon ash) **w**
Lithocarpus densiflorus (tanbark oak) **w**
Populus spp. (poplar, cottonwood,
  aspen)
  tremuloides (quaking aspen)
  trichocarpa (cottonwood)
Prunus
  emarginata (bitter cherry)
  pensylvanica (pie cherry,
  bird cherry)
  virginiana demissa (chokecherry) **E**
Quercus (oak)
  chrysolepis* (canyon live oak) **w**
  Garryana (Garry oak) **w**
  Kelloggii (California black oak) **w**
Rhamnus purshiana (cascara,
  cascara sagrada)
Sambucus (elderberry)
  cerulea (blue elderberry)
  racemosa (red elderberry)
Umbellularia californica* (California bay
  laurel, Oregon myrtle) **w**

SHRUBS

Chrysothamnus nauseosus (rabbitbush)
Cornus stolonifera* (red osier dogwood)
Corylus cornuta (hazelnut)
Gaultheria shallon* (salal) **w**
Holodiscus discolor* (ocean spray)
Mahonia aquifolium* (Oregon grape)
Myrica
  californica* (Pacific wax myrtle) **w**
  gale (sweet gale) **w**
Osmaronia cerasiformis (Indian plum,
  osoberry)
Pachistima myrsinites* (Oregon
  boxwood)
Potentilla fruticosa* (cinquefoil)
Rhus glabra (sumac)
Ribes
  aureum (yellow currant)
  sanguineum (red flowering currant)
Rosa (rose)
  nutkana (Nootka rose)
  Woodsii (Wood's rose)
Rubus
  parviflorus (thimbleberry)
  spectabilis (salmonberry)
Shepherdia*
  argentea* (soapberry, soopollalie) **E**
  canadensis* (buffaloberry) **E**
Vaccinium ovatum* (evergreen
  huckleberry) **w**
Viburnum
  edule (low bush cranberry)
  opulus* (high bush cranberry)

GROUNDCOVERS

Arctostaphylos*
  x *media*
  uva-ursi (kinnikinnick)
Cassiope Mertensiana (white moss
  heather) **w**
Cornus canadensis* (bunchberry)
Dicentra formosa* (bleeding heart)
Empetrum nigrum (crowberry)
Fragaria (strawberry)
  chiloensis* (coastal strawberry—
  shiny dark leaves)
  virginiana (wild strawberry—
  gray-green leaves)
Juniperus communis (common juniper
  varieties)
Linnaea borealis (twinflower)
Luetkea pectinata (Alaska spirea,
  partridgefoot)
Mahonia nervosa* (Cascade
  Oregon grape)
Maianthemum dilatatum* (false
  lily-of-the-valley)
Oxalis oregana* (wood sorrel) **w**
Phyllodoce empetriformis (red
  mountain heather) **w**
Rubus
  chamaemorus (cloudberry)
  pedatus (trailing raspberry,
  strawberry bramble)
Vaccinium
  oxycoccus (true cranberry)
  vitis-idaea* (lingonberry)

READING LIST

This annotated reading list of books and magazines contains titles that will be useful to people interested in gardens and landscaping. You might also want to look for special-topic book series from HP Books (Los Angeles: Price Stern Sloan), Ortho Books (San Francisco), and Sunset Books (Menlo Park, Calif.: Lane Publishing).

BOOKS

Barton, Barbara J. *Gardening by Mail: A Source Book*. Boston: Houghton Mifflin Company, 1990. *The* source catalog for seed, plant, and garden tool companies. I tried to think of a reputable horticultural firm Ms. Barton doesn't list, but I failed; she knows all my suppliers, famous and obscure, here and abroad.

Clifford, Derek. *A History of Garden Design*. New York: Frederick A. Prager, 1963. A fine study of why we make gardens. Clifford is opinionated and fun to read.

Creasy, Rosalind. *Complete Book of Edible Landscaping*. San Francisco: Sierra Club Press, 1982.

Fleming, Laurence, and Alan Gore. *The English Garden*. London: Michael Joseph, 1979. An amusing and informative historical look at the English garden.

Grant, John A., and Carol L. Grant. *Garden Design Illustrated*. Seattle: University of Washington Press, 1954. A classic guide to landscape design, of special interest to the Northwest because of its emphasis on plants and themes that do well here. Out of print, but check your library.

Harrison, Charles R. *Ornamental Conifers*. New York: Hafner Press/Macmillan Publishing Co., 1975. Over 500 photographs and accompanying descriptions of conifers, most of them suitable for at least some areas of the Northwest.

Hilliers' Manual of Trees & Shrubs. Newton Abbot, Devon, U.K.: David & Charles, 1975. A plant catalog of material sold by Hillier and Sons nursery in England. The descriptions are not overly technical in detail, making this a good introduction to rare plants for enthusiasts.

Japan Exterior Group, eds. *New Way to Garden*. Tokyo: Nihonbungei. Written in Japanese, but filled with easy-to-interpret drawings of Japanese landscape ideas.

Kourik, Robert. *Designing and Maintaining Your Edible Landscape Naturally*. Emmaeus, Penn.: Metamorphic Press/Rodale, 1986. Recommended for people interested in maximizing food production within an attractive landscape.

Kress, Stephen W. *Audubon Society Guide to Attracting Birds*. New York: Scribners, 1985. Tells what plants and ruses will attract specific birds to your yard.

Kruckeberg, Arthur R. *Gardening with Native Plants of the Pacific Northwest*. Seattle: University of Washington Press, 1982. The standard guide for anyone using native plants.

Liberty Hyde Bailey Hortorium. *Hortus Third: A Concise Dictionary of Plants Cultivated in the United States and Canada*. New York: Macmillan Publishing Co., 1976. Precise botanical descriptions of over 20,000 plants grown in American gardens. Of more interest to plant enthusiasts than casual browsers.

Lovejoy, Ann. *The Year in Bloom: Gardening for All Seasons in the Pacific Northwest*. Seattle: Sasquatch Books, 1987. Examines the horticultural wealth that our region can draw upon for year-round color.

Lyons, C. P. *Trees, Shrubs and Flowers to Know in Washington.* Toronto: J. M. Dent & Sons Ltd., 1956. This volume is small enough to take with you on nature hikes. It includes range maps showing where the trees listed occur naturally, plus close-ups and overall drawings of trees and plants.

Saito, Katsuo, and Sadaji Wada. *Magic of Trees and Stone: Secrets of Japanese Gardening.* New York: JPT Book Company, 1964.

Schenk, George. *How to Plan, Establish, and Maintain Rock Gardens.* Menlo Park, Calif.: Lane Publishing Co., 1964. Not currently in print, this is worth seeking out in libraries.

——— *The Complete Shade Gardener.* Boston: Houghton Mifflin Company, 1984. A clear discussion of the opportunities available to shade gardeners.

Schofield, Janice J. *Discovering Wild Plants: Alaska, Western Canada, the Northwest.* Anchorage and Seattle: Alaska Northwest Books, 1989. Clear color photographs and line drawings supplement a careful study of Western plants used for food and medicine.

Solomon, Steve. *Growing Vegetables West of the Cascades.* Seattle: Sasquatch Books, 1989. A detailed study of vegetable culture for the Pacific Northwest, with fine information about soil types, pest control, and recommended crops, by the former owner of Territorial Seed Company.

Sunset Western Garden Book. Menlo Park, Calif.: Lane Publishing Co., 1988. This has useful plant zone maps and gardening information, but I find it especially interesting for its plant dictionary section.

Turnbull, Cass. *The Complete Guide to Landscape Design, Renovation, and Maintenance.* Crozet, Va.: BetterWay Publications, 1991. From the founder of PlantAmnesty, this book concentrates on the art of maintenance.

University of British Columbia Botanical Garden. *UBC Guide to Gardening in British Columbia.* Vancouver, B.C.: University of British Columbia Press, 1990. A large, comprehensive gardening book suitable for gardeners in western Canada and the northwestern United States.

Veblen, Thorstein. *Theory of the Leisure Class.* Boston: Houghton Mifflin Company, 1973. A section of this book examines origins of garden traditions, including large lawns.

Welch, Humphrey J. *Manual of Dwarf Conifers.* New York: Theophrastus Publishers, 1979. Contains a dictionary section and a photograph section to help describe hundreds of useful dwarf conifers.

MAGAZINES

Brooklyn Botanic Garden Record, Plants & Gardens (Brooklyn, N.Y.: Brooklyn Botanic Garden). Each issue is devoted to a particular plant or gardening topic.

Garden Design (Washington, D.C.: Evergreen Publishing).

Gardens West (Vancouver, B.C.: Cornwall Publishing). A garden magazine focusing on Western Canada.

Landscape Architecture (Washington, D.C.: American Society of Landscape Architects). For landscape professionals and dedicated amateurs interested in theoretical, historical, and practical aspects of landscaping.

Organic Gardening (Emmaeus, Penn.: Rodale Publishing). A practical guide to reliable old methods and promising new techniques in gardening without chemicals.

Pacific Horticulture (San Francisco: Pacific Horticultural Foundation). No one may bother me when I'm reading this. A treasure.

Sunset (Menlo Park, Calif.: Lane Publishing Co.). The magazine includes landscape success stories and gardening advice tailored to specific regions in the West.

INDEX

Many other fascinating books are available from Alaska Northwest Books™.
Ask for them at your favorite bookstore, or write us for a complete free catalog.

Alaska Northwest Books™
A division of GTE Discovery Publications
P.O. Box 3007, Bothell, WA 98041-3007, 1-800-343-4567